EVY: GEORGE FREDERIC WATTS'S PORTRAIT OF EVELEEN TENNANT

KEDRUN LAURIE | OCCASIONAL PAPER 5

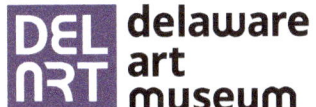

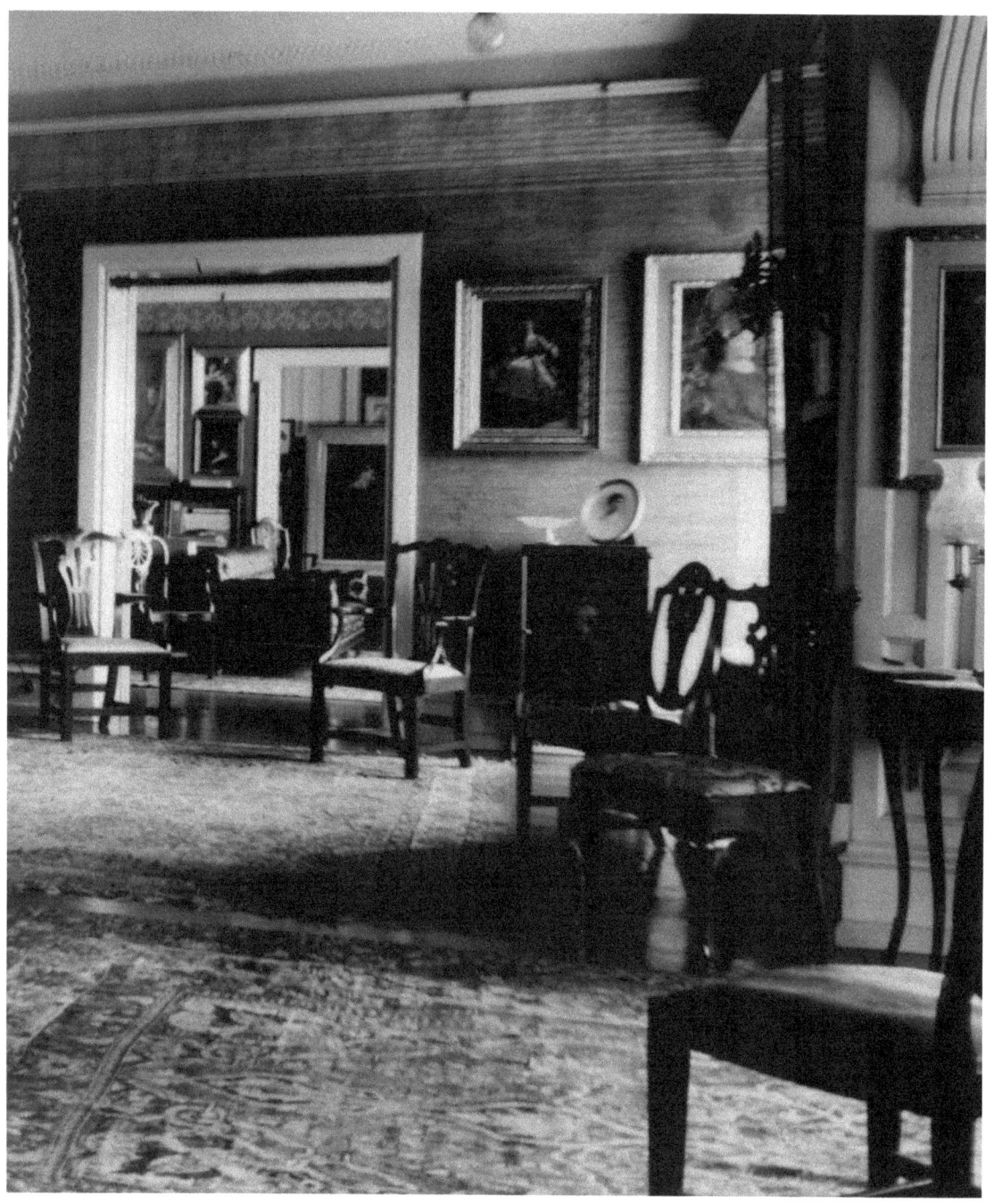

Library of Congress Control Number: 2021912935

ISBN: 978-1-7367899-1-9

A publication of the Delaware Art Museum/©Kedrun Laurie

CONTENTS

Acknowledgments 7

List of Illustrations 8

Preface 9

Evy: George Frederic Watts's Portrait of Eveleen Tennant 11

Archival Sources 51

Abbreviations 52

Notes 52

Bibliography 65

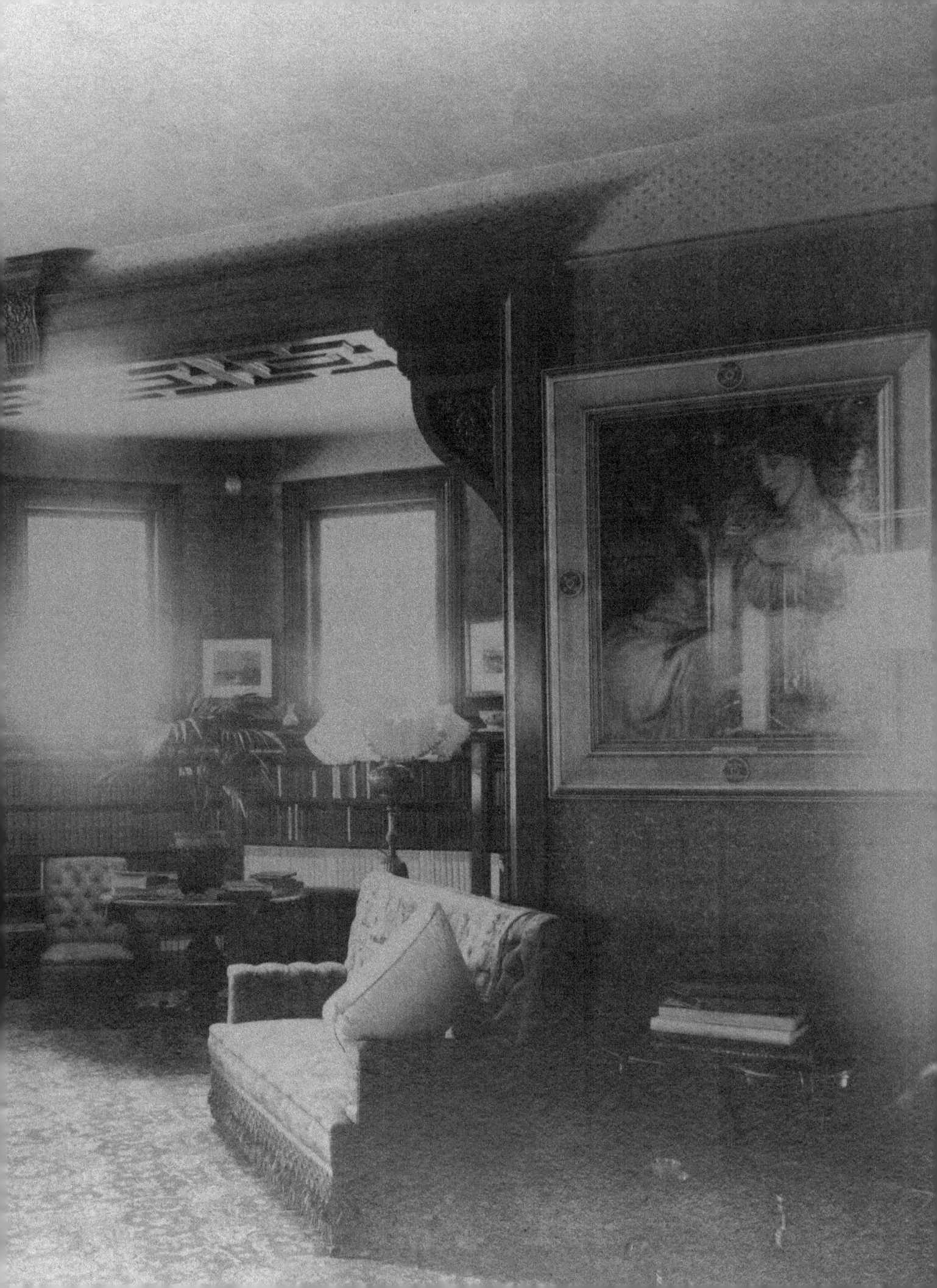

EVY: GEORGE FREDERIC WATTS'S PORTRAIT OF EVELEEN TENNANT

KEDRUN LAURIE | OCCASIONAL PAPER 5

ACKNOWLEDGMENTS

My warmest thanks above all to Margaretta S. Frederick, the Annette Woolard-Provine Curator of the Bancroft Pre-Raphaelite Collection at the Delaware Art Museum, but also to my family—Nicholas, Harriet, and Rafe Martyn—for their superb support.

I wish to acknowledge the scholarship of David Waller and Trevor Hamilton, whose work preceded mine and made it infinitely easier.

I extend my gratitude for their generous help in many areas to:
Georgia Atienza, National Portrait Gallery, London
Beatrice Bertram, Watts Gallery, Compton
Revd James Buxton, Corpus Christi College, Cambridge
Sarah Colborne and Hayley Cotterill, Manuscripts and Special Collections, University of Nottingham
Elizabeth Denholm, Delaware Art Museum
Rachael DiEleuterio, Delaware Art Museum
Lucy Hughes, Corpus Christi College, Cambridge
James Kirwan, Wren Library, Trinity College, Cambridge
Isabelle de Lannoy
Abbie Latham, Watts Gallery
Gosia Lawik, Country Orders, London Library
Mathilde Leduc-Grimaldi, Henry M. Stanley Archive, Royal Museum for Central Africa, Tervuren, Belgium
Leonée Ormond
Nicholas Tromans
David Waller
Hannah Williamson, Manchester Art Gallery
Margaret Winslow, Delaware Art Museum

My final thanks go to Mark Bockrath of Barbara A. Buckley & Associates for his technical report on the painting and to Gretchen Dykstra and Cynthia Oswald for their editing and designing of the book.

LIST OF ILLUSTRATIONS

COVER

George Frederic Watts, Portrait of Eveleen Tennant (later Mrs. F. W. H. Myers), 1876–79. Oil on canvas. 641 × 514 mm. Delaware Art Museum, Samuel and Mary R. Bancroft Memorial.

IN TEXT

Fig. 1. George Frederic Watts, *Eveleen Tennant, later Mrs. F. W. H. Myers*, 1876–[?]80. Oil on canvas. 1003 × 711 mm. Photo © Tate.

Fig. 2. George Frederic Watts, *Dorothy Tennant*, 1876–77. Oil on wood. 635 × 533 mm. Photo © Tate.

Fig. 3. Eveleen Myers (née Tennant), *Gertrude Barbara Rich Tennant (née Collier)*, 1890s. Platinum print. 212 × 163 mm. © National Portrait Gallery, London.

Fig. 4. Unknown photographer, *Charles Tennant*, 1860s. Albumen print. 90 × 55 mm. © National Portrait Gallery, London.

Fig. 5. John Everett Millais, *Miss Eveleen Tennant*, 1874. Oil on canvas. 1079 × 800 mm. Photo © Tate.

Fig. 6. Unknown, French painter, *Charles Brinsley Marlay*, c. 1850. Oil on canvas. 673 × 559 mm. © The Fitzwilliam Museum, Cambridge.

Fig. 7. George Frederic Watts, *Portrait of Eveleen Tennant (later Mrs. F. W. H. Myers)*, 1876–79. Oil on canvas. 641 × 514 mm. Delaware Art Museum, Samuel and Mary R. Bancroft Memorial.

Fig. 8. Julia Margaret Cameron, *[A Bacchante]*, June 20, 1867. Albumen silver print. 251 × 200 mm. *The J. Paul Getty Museum, Los Angeles*. Digital image courtesy of the Getty's Open Content Program.

Fig. 9. [After a drawing by Frank Miles], *Eveleen Myers (née Tennant) as Vanessa*, 1875–76. 137 × 110 mm. © National Portrait Gallery, London.

Fig. 10. George Frederic Watts, *The Seamstress or The Song of the Shirt*, 1850. Oil on canvas. 1448 × 1270 mm. © Watts Gallery/© Trustees of Watts Gallery/Bridgeman

Fig. 11. Eveleen Myers (née Tennant), *Frederic William Henry Myers*, c. 1890. Platinum print. 251 × 200 mm. © National Portrait Gallery, London.

Fig. 12. George Frederic Watts, *Self-Portrait*, 1864. Oil on canvas. 648 × 521 mm. Photo © Tate.

Fig. 13. Edward Bringhurst. *Drawing Room in Rockford, Home of Samuel Bancroft Jr.*, 1937. Samuel and Mary R. Bancroft Pre-Raphaelite Manuscript Collection, Helen Farr Sloan Library and Archives, Delaware Art Museum.

Fig. 14. John Everett Millais, *The White Cockade*, 1862. Oil on panel. 610 × 451 mm. Delaware Art Museum, Samuel and Mary R. Bancroft Memorial.

Fig. 15. Dante Gabriel Rossetti, *Lady Lilith*, 1866–68 (altered 1872–73). Oil on canvas. 991 × 864 mm. Delaware Art Museum, Samuel and Mary R. Bancroft Memorial.

Fig. 16. Unknown photographer. *Drawing Room Alcove in Rockford, Home of Samuel Bancroft, Jr.*, c. 1893. Samuel and Mary R. Bancroft Pre-Raphaelite Manuscript Collection, Helen Farr Sloan Library and Archives, Delaware Art Museum. *Lady Lilith* by Dante Gabriel Rossetti hanging at right.

Fig. 17. Eveleen Myers (née Tennant), *Adelaide Augusta Floyd Passingham (1867-1954)*, 1889. Platinum print. 293 × 222 mm. © National Portrait Gallery, London.

Fig. 18. Eveleen Myers (née Tennant), *Leonora Piper*, 1890. Platinum print. 275 × 225 mm. © National Portrait Gallery, London.

Fig. 19. Eveleen Myers (née Tennant), *Albert George Dew-Smith*, 1888. Albumen print. 170 × 145 mm. © National Portrait Gallery, London.

PREFACE

This publication follows a decades old, if sporadic, tradition initiated in 1976 under the auspices of then Associate Director and Chief Curator Rowland Elzea. The concept was and is still to provide a platform for expanding our knowledge of individual works or particular strengths of the Museum's collection and archives. We are particularly grateful for the assistance of the Clark Family Foundation in support of this volume.

The Museum's Samuel and Mary R. Bancroft Collection of Pre-Raphaelite Art came about in 1935 through the gift of the widow and son of the collector, Samuel Bancroft (1840–1915). The works of art were offered to the nascent Wilmington Society of Fine Arts along with a gift of land on which the current building now stands. Samuel Bancroft's taste for the Pre-Raphaelites was unique in the United States, during a period in which French academic and early impressionist painting were more widely acquired. His defiance of societal conceits and tenacity in pursuit of his passion for this overlooked moment in British art was undoubtedly bolstered by a personality described as "fearless as to what others might say or think." His zeal for the art and culture of the period included both intensive art collecting over a relatively short period of time (1890–1914) and a rigorous program of self-education, evident in the substantial library and archives that were part of the 1935 gift.

The acquisition of G. F. Watts's *Portrait of Eveleen Tennant* (1876-1879), the subject of this volume, occurred around the midpoint of his campaign of acquisition. At the time, Bancroft was working closely with London art dealers Thomas Agnew and Sons, as well as Pre-Raphaelite artist, connoisseur, and collector Charles Fairfax Murray. In 1900, when the portrait entered Bancroft's collection, it joined benchmark works such as Dante Gabriel Rossetti's *Water Willow* (1871) and *Lady Lilith* (1866-8; altered 1872-3) as well as Edward Burne-Jones's *The Council Chamber* (c. 1872-1892). The collector's knowledge of the period accompanied by a burgeoning self-confidence in his acumen was such that a frustrated Fairfax Murray responded to one of his many suppositions as "wholly imaginary and impossible."[1]

Nonetheless, Bancroft would have found Kedrun Laurie's comprehensive and original interpretation of Watts's rendering of pioneering art photographer Eveleen Tennant (later Mrs. F.W.H. Myers) fascinating. Dr. Laurie's thorough parsing out of the people and places integral to its creation provide a much-needed context for this understudied but important portrait. She imparts clarification for the puzzling date, a detail questioned by Bancroft himself. With the aid of recent conservation analysis, thanks to the efforts of Mark Bockrath and Barbara Buckley, Laurie builds a strong case for the chronological development of the painting, while simultaneously substantiating the motives of those closely associated with it. The result is an important piece of scholarship and an engrossing story.

When I came to the Museum in 2003, I found myself thankful to have access to the notes and documentation left to me by Elzea, who was, for all intents and purposes, the collection's first modern curator. From my earliest days it has been a particular wish of mine to continue the Occasional Paper series he started and honor his good work. My thanks to Dr. Laurie for generously sharing her research for this publication and for making this most recent addition to the series possible.

Margaretta S. Frederick
Annette Woolard-Provine Curator
of the Bancroft Pre-Raphaelite Collection
May 14, 2021

NOTE

[1] Letter, Fairfax Murray to Bancroft, September 11, 1899, Rowland Elzea, ed. Delaware Art Museum Occasional Paper, no. 2 (February 1980): 162.

EVY: GEORGE FREDERIC WATTS'S PORTRAIT OF EVELEEN TENNANT

Kedrun Laurie

The Delaware Art Museum's *Portrait of Eveleen Tennant (Later Mrs. F.W.H. Myers)* presents an image of a rather watchful young girl in a high-necked scarlet dress. A tawny cloak covers the chair on which she sits. A bank of red flowers and green foliage frames her dark hair, which is starred with white blossom. Her shining face is filled with light, although the sky itself is clouded and sombre. The girl is Eveleen Tennant (1856–1937) and the painter George Frederic Watts (1817–1904). Although a relatively little-known work by the great Victorian artist, it has a complex history, one which this publication will tell, interleaving it with the no-less-fascinating biography of Eveleen herself.[1]

The picture came to the United States in 1900 after Watts finally decided to part with a work of which he was as fond as he was of its sitter. Samuel J. Bancroft Jr. (1840–1915) of the Delaware firm of cotton-finishers, bought it from Agnew's, the art dealers, during a trip to London, and hung it in the drawing room of Rockford, his home in Wilmington. His descendants bequeathed it to the Museum, with the rest of his outstanding Pre-Raphaelite art collection, in 1935.

EVY AND DOLLY

Watts had begun two portraits of Eveleen Tennant on the Isle of Wight in September 1876. In the first, which belongs to the Tate Gallery (fig. 1), she is again wearing red, but this time holds a reddish-brown umbrella to protect herself from the darkening sky. In the background is the cliff edge and the sea. Although larger and very different in character from the second, it has the same title. I will therefore call the two works the Tate and the Delaware portraits to distinguish them from each other. Toward the end of September, Watts also began a painting of Eveleen's elder sister, Dorothy (1855–1926): *Miss Dorothy Tennant, Second Daughter of the Late Charles Tennant, Esq, of Cadoxton Lodge, Neath, Glamorganshire* (fig. 2).

The sisters were eccentric, exuberant characters and not in the least conventional. In the late 1880s Eveleen would become a fine portrait photographer, while Dorothy, who trained as an artist, exhibited regularly and above all wrote compellingly. Their marriages were noteworthy, if a little off beam. In 1880 Eveleen wed Cambridge classicist, poet, and psychical researcher Frederic Myers (1843–1901) and ten years later, in 1890, Dorothy united herself to the famous explorer of Central Africa, Henry Morton Stanley (1841–1904).

When Watts began his portraits of them, Eveleen (Evy, or sometimes Evie) Tennant was nineteen,

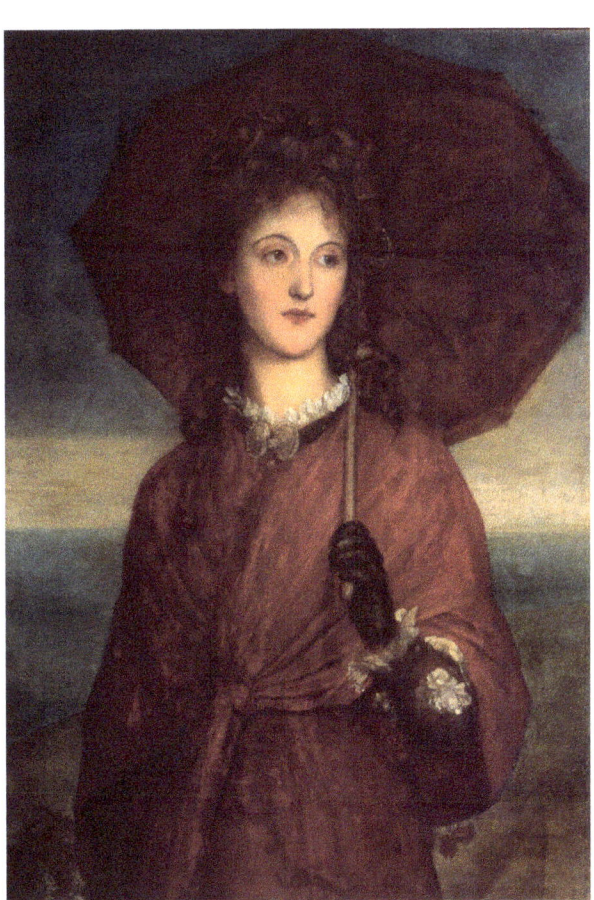

Fig. 1. George Frederic Watts, *Eveleen Tennant, Later Mrs. F.W.H. Myers*, 1876–?1880, oil on canvas, 1003 x 711 mm, Tate, London, N05116

FACING: Detail George Frederic Watts, *Portrait of Eveleen Tennant (later Mrs. F.W.H. Myers)*, 1876–1879, oil on canvas, 641 x 514 mm, Delaware Art Museum, Samuel and Mary R. Bancroft Memorial, 1935-34

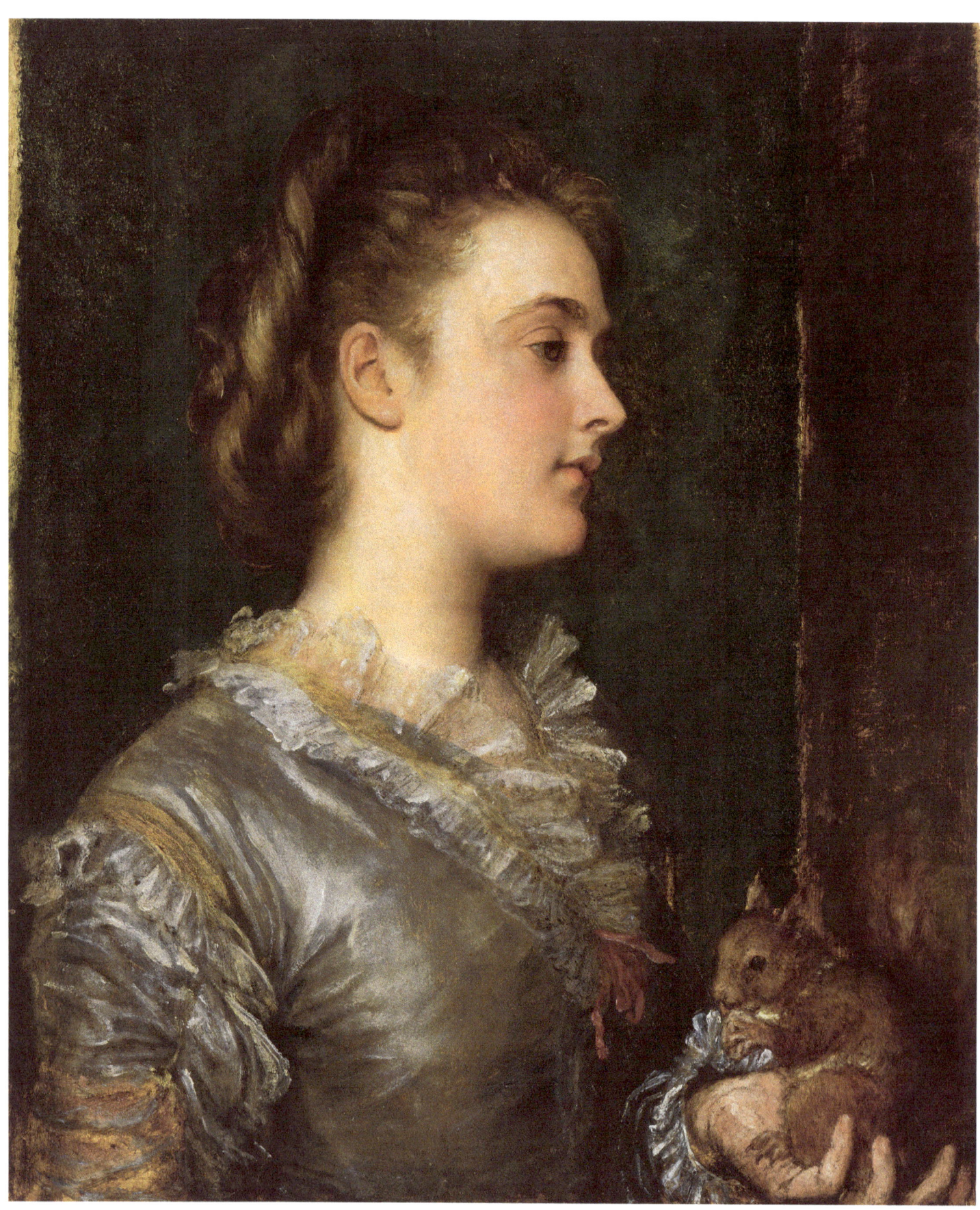

Fig. 2. George Frederic Watts, *Miss Dorothy Tennant, Second Daughter of the Late Charles Tennant, Esq, of Cadoxton Lodge, Neath, Glamorganshire*, 1876–1877, oil on wood, 635 x 533 mm, Tate, London, N04223

and Dorothy (always known as Dolly) was twenty-one.² They were the youngest surviving children of Gertrude Tennant, née Collier (1819–1918, fig. 3) and lawyer and former Member of Parliament Charles Tennant (1796–1873, fig. 4), of Cadoxton Lodge, Glamorgan.³

In his lifetime Tennant had been a cautious, conservative man of Radical political views. His wealth derived from his Welsh estates and the Tennant Canal. Opened by his father in 1824, this was the second largest private canal in Britain, carrying coal to Swansea, ironstone to the ironworks at Neath Abbey and saltpeter and brimstone to the gunpowder manufactory at Glynneath.⁴ Gertrude had to work hard to keep it profitable after Charles's death, in the face of stiff competition from the railways, but was aided by the fact that her husband had prudently taken out shares in the Neath and Brecon Railway Company and made considerable investments elsewhere.⁵ The family thus had a substantial if not vast income. They were town gentry in London and landed gentry in Wales. In neither place, however, were they quite as firmly established as they wished to be. This sense of being somewhat on the fringes of the Establishment gave them a distinct sympathy for the poor, yet they never ceased to aspire socially. As a family they looked both ways.

Charles's death on March 10, 1873 devastated the family, and Gertrude and Dolly vowed respectively to remain "spotless" and "unspotted" until their reunion with him in heaven.⁶ Dolly began to keep a journal addressed to the dead man, which she continued in intimate detail for years, even after her marriage to Stanley. The twenty-one manuscript volumes were marked forbiddingly around the edges, "PRIVATE / PERSONAL / SACRED," for self-advertisement was contrary to Dolly's Puritan nature and these writings were meant only for her deceased father's eyes. Her father's all-seeing gaze from the afterlife was to Dolly more real than any living person's and certainly any living artist's view of her.

The journals describe in vivid detail the painting of the portraits of the sisters and it is mainly thanks to a study of them that I have been able to expand upon the history of the Delaware portrait of Eveleen Tennant.⁷

After her husband's death, Gertrude ran, with growing confidence, a Paris-style salon at 2 Richmond Terrace, Westminster. This rented townhouse, a step away from the British Houses of Parliament, had been the family home since 1868. The tone of the salon was set by women, Gertrude being actively assisted by her bright, lively daughters, including the eldest, Alice, or Elsie (1848–1930). Although her "mopy— or knagging" behavior was a severe trial to the others, Elsie was not hidden away but fully involved on social occasions.⁸ Dolly later learnt to call this sister's mental health problems "hysteria."⁹ Charles, or Charlie (1852–1928), the only son, in any event a less animated character, was away at Oxford until 1876. "[H]aving no man, getting on in London is hard, although we have been very successful," wrote Dolly that year.¹⁰

Gertrude's salon also derived its character from its location near Whitehall. She could invite the foremost politicians of the day, from William Gladstone himself to Radical MP and former miner Thomas Burt, to call in for lunch, tea, dinner, or an evening party on their way back from the House. Writers, actors, and artists such as Edward Burne-Jones and Henry Irving were added to the mix. A third and no less vital ingredient was the French one, again consisting of politicians and diplomats, writers, artists and actors. Having been brought up in France, where her father had fled in 1825 to avoid bankruptcy, Gertrude encouraged her own children to be bilingual and expected her guests to operate in two languages if possible and to mingle for mutual benefit and understanding.¹¹

Genuine hospitality and intellectual curiosity aside, there was another aspect to Gertrude's entertaining, and that was the need to settle her fatherless children. Among her husband's last words to her had been the injunction: "Be prudent

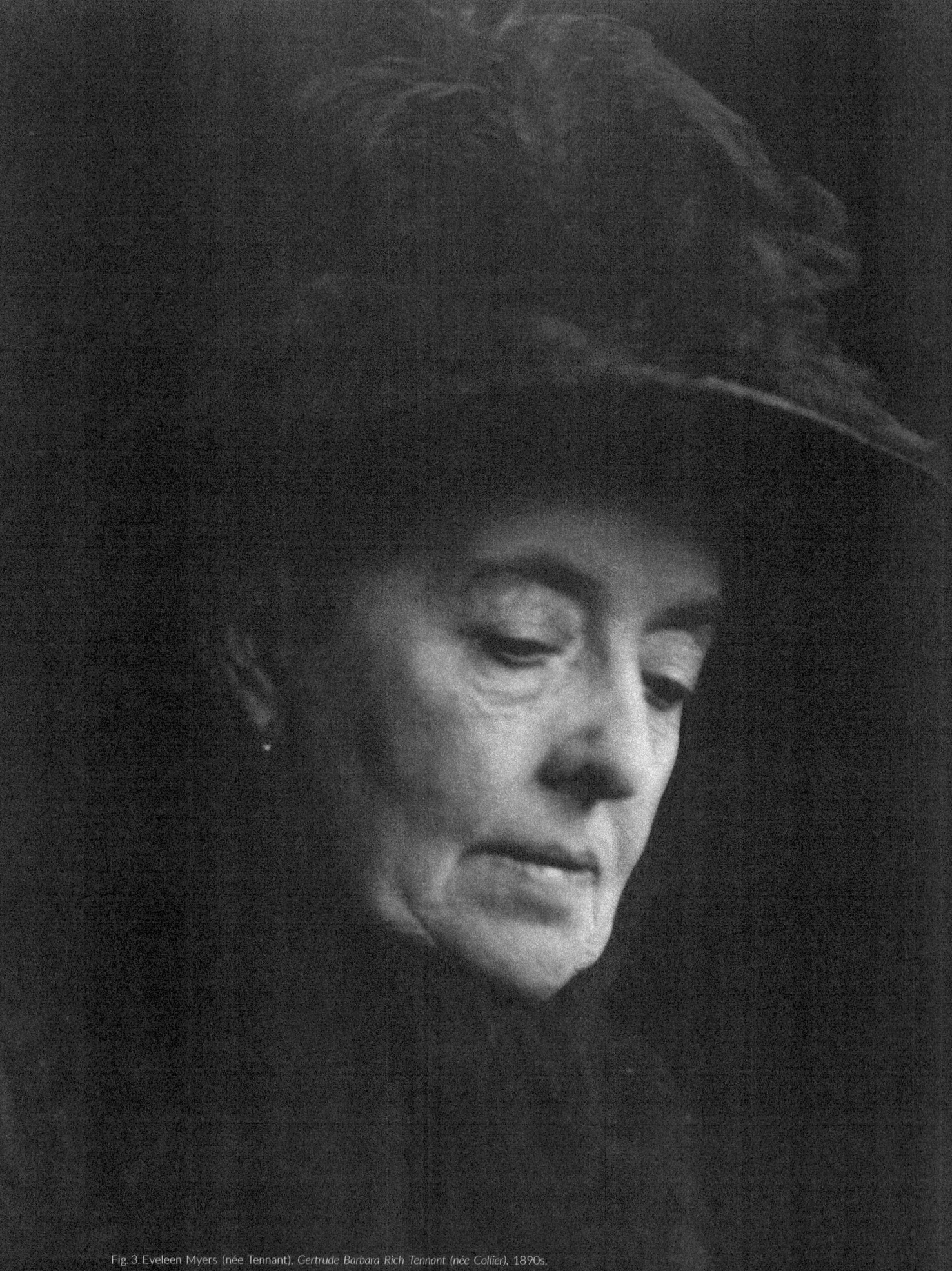

Fig. 3. Eveleen Myers (née Tennant), *Gertrude Barbara Rich Tennant (née Collier)*, 1890s, platinum print, 212 x 163 mm, National Portrait Gallery, London, NPG Ax68562

and economical and don't get into debt, you have not a friend in the world who can help you if you do."[12] Gertrude took this advice extremely seriously and trained herself to be an impressive financial manager. She was not concerned about Charlie, who had since 1866 been provided for under the will of a friend of his father. Although he ultimately became a lawyer, he was at this point destined for a political career and sent to Harrow and Balliol. Her home-tutored daughters, however, even Dolly, who was self-confessedly far more interested in politics then her brother, were meant to find husbands who would consolidate or better still enhance the family's social standing and provide for them financially after their mother's death.

Gertrude was immensely proud of her daughters and wanted them to have husbands who were worthy of them. She called on all the great names in her formidable address book to act as mentors. In 1871, possibly on the recommendation of Frederic Leighton, whose protégé he was, both Dolly and Evy began art lessons with Italian painter Carlo Perugini, though these soon had to end as they were too expensive.[13] Evy drew well, but it would be Dolly who went on to become the artist, from 1871 to 1879 attending the Slade School of Art as one of its first women students.[14] Evy had real musical ability, playing the piano and the guitar.[15] Above all she was noted for her beautiful soprano voice, made, according to Dolly into "the wonderful organ it really is" by H. C. Deacon, a singing-master of Wimpole Street who was afterward on the staff of the Royal College of Music.[16] In 1876 she became a member of the Guild of Amateur Musicians, whose conductor Henry Leslie, founder two years later of the precursor to the Royal College, pronounced her "the finest soprano he ever heard in an amateur."[17] In May of that year, in Paris with her mother and Dolly, Eveleen was invited to sing to renowned French mezzo-soprano Pauline Viardot at her house, the introduction having been effected by

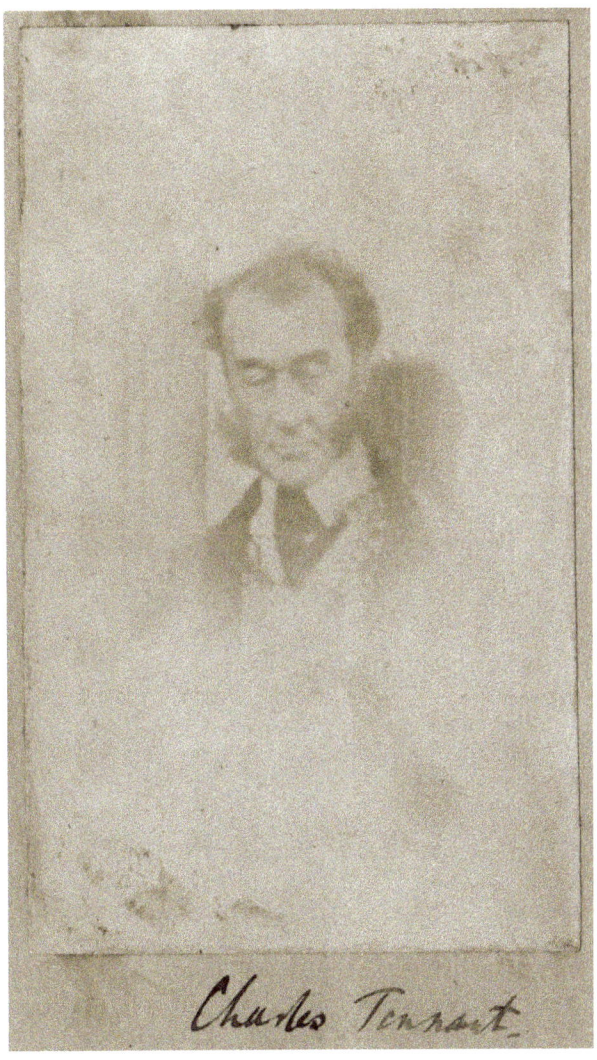

Fig. 4. Photographer unknown, *Charles Tennant*, 1860s, albumen print, 90 x 55 mm, National Portrait Gallery, London, NPG Ax68309

Gertrude's old friend Gustave Flaubert.[18] Four years later, in January 1880, when Émile Durand-Gréville, the art critic and translator of Turgenev, met the Tennants through the painter Jean-Jacques Henner, Evy was still being described as Mme Viardot's pupil. Durand-Gréville's comments on her then were a little dry, "L'une des filles, aux traits fins et énergiques, aux cheveux noirs un peu en désordre, chante, avec un vrai sentiment, sinon avec méthode; elle est élève de Mme Viardot."[19]

Her granddaughter Deenagh Goold-Adams's reaction to Evy's singing, many years later, was also somewhat mixed:

My earliest memory of my grandmother is of her singing lullabies to me in my nursery (about 1921). This was done with what seemed to me an embarrassing excess of feeling and a tremolo voice which made my inside quake. She had a great tendency to burst into song and painful as it was to me in the 1920s I am sure that in the 1880s she sang very prettily and with considerable élan.[20]

Back in London in June 1876, however, Dolly noted that at Lord and Lady Petersham's: "Eveleen sang to the delight and astonishment of everyone as her voice, fine as it was has very much improved."[21] Evy's singing was deployed not only to entertain her mother's friends and guests, but also to advertise her attractiveness and marriageability. Although Dolly, and no doubt Evy, disliked such connotations, there was no avoiding the hard reality that their talents were being used as commodities in the marriage market. We hear much less about Evy's singing after her marriage, which arrested its development at amateur level, while the man she wed is reputed to have had little feel for music.[22]

MYERS PURSUES EVELEEN

In purely mercantile terms Eveleen had an advantage over Dolly that her elder sister generously recognized, and that was her greater beauty. This winning tool was one that Gertrude used to full advantage by having her youngest daughter's portrait painted as often as possible. Her old friend John Everett Millais (1829–1896), the pre-eminent society portraitist of the day, assisted her by making a magnificent, massive likeness of Eveleen in 1874 (fig. 5) and a secondary one of Dolly, less helpfully entitled *No!*, in 1875. The paintings and their sitters became the sensations of the 1875 Academy, Eveleen's changing the course of her life when it was seen by the man she was to marry, Frederic Myers. Visiting the exhibition with the woman he loved, his cousin's wife Annie Marshall, Myers persuaded himself that a psychic charge had passed from the innocent eyes of Eveleen's portrait to his and Annie's, connecting them mystically and almost erotically, his and Annie's love having remained decently unconsummated.[23] Myers met Eveleen in person for the first time nearly a year later, on February 6, 1876, at George Eliot's, when, as she tells us, considering it a significant detail, her "hair was down."[24] She was nineteen, and girls' hair was generally up by this stage, as the puritanical Dolly preferred hers to be, but Eveleen, more expressive and less constrained than her sister, liked hers down.

In August 1876 Annie drowned herself. The grieving Myers came to believe that because of the episode in front of her portrait at the Academy Eveleen could somehow put him in contact with Annie's spirit. He found her again on November 14, 1879, at a late evening musical party to which he had been invited by Gertrude's cousin, the playwright and author Hamilton Aïdé.[25] On Saturday, November 29, he sat next to Dolly at a dinner party at Aïdé's, also attended by Eveleen. In his diary entry for Sunday, November 30, the word "Tennants" is underlined.[26] On December 4, Myers sent Dolly his article on Virgil from the *Fortnightly Review* that they had been discussing on the twenty-ninth.[27] On December 5, 1879, Gertrude and her daughters went to Paris.[28] On December 15, Myers wrote to Dolly again. Having found that he was to be in Paris on business of friends of his mother's, he wondered if he might call on them.[29] On the twentieth, according to his diary, he went to Paris and on the twenty-first called at their hotel, the Hotel de France et de Bath in the rue Saint-Honoré. Afterward he saw them daily and on Christmas Eve took the girls to the Sainte-Chapelle, where he gave them letters in the form of acrostics, Dolly's about art and Eveleen's expressing passionate love.[30] Eveleen failed to recognize his declaration as such and so at the Louvre on December 27, Gertrude again absent,

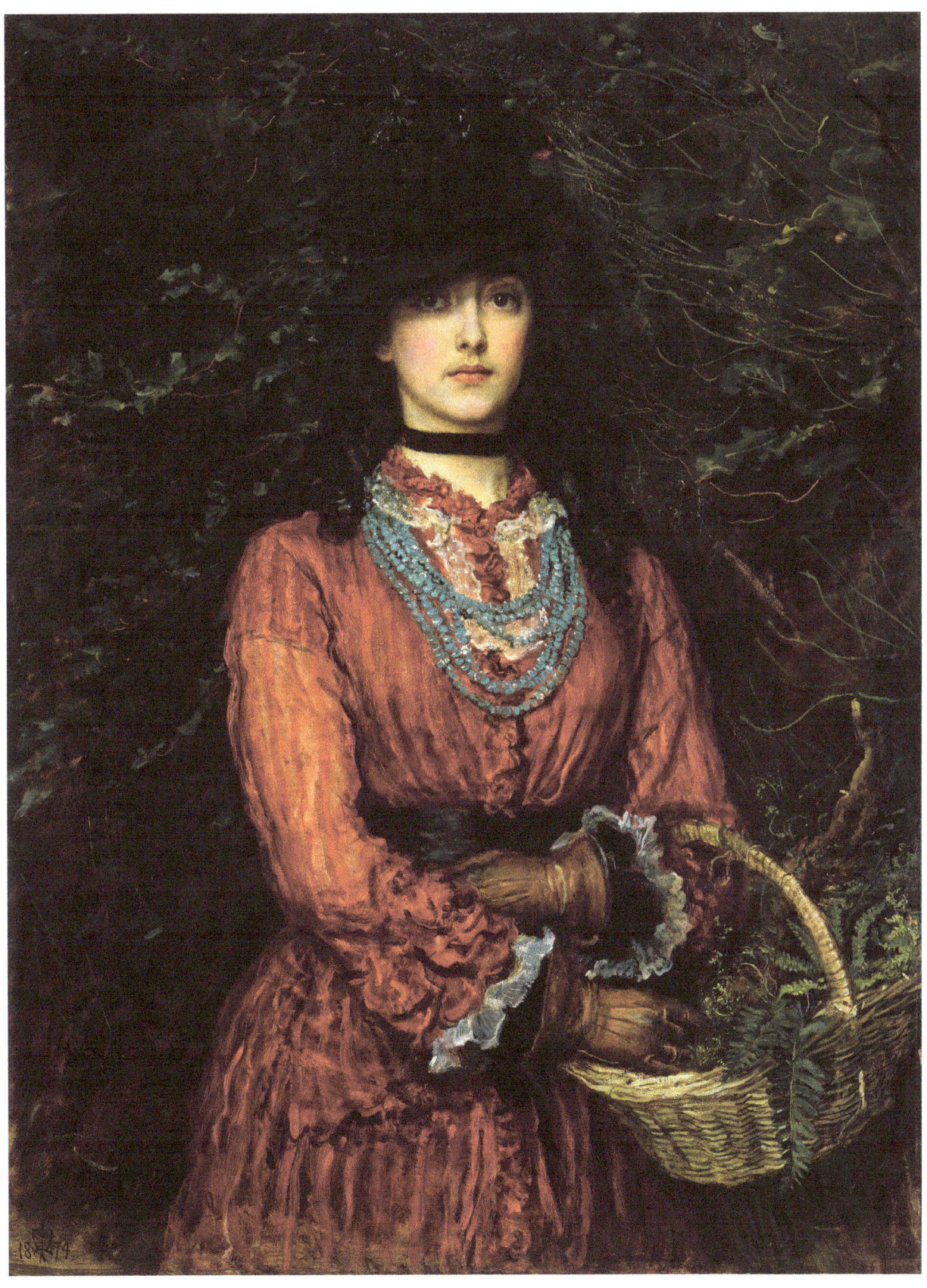

Fig. 5. John Everett Millais, *Miss Eveleen Tennant*, 1874, oil on canvas, 1079 x 800 mm (support), Tate, London, N05260

and Dolly of the party but somehow eluded, Myers proposed to her again, in less obscure a manner, and she accepted him. This was a shock to all who knew Eveleen. In mid-February the novelist Henry James, who had first met Gertrude in 1877 and was friendly with the girls too, confessed to Mrs. Tennant that although he had observed Eveleen in Paris (he was briefly there at the same time as them), he had had no inkling of what was to come, "I was not conscious of her [Eveleen's] little affair being 'in the air' in Paris, & yet I fancy myself an observer. After this I shall abandon the pretention."[31] Very soon afterward, on March 10, 1880, Myers and Eveleen were married in the Lady Chapel of Henry VII at Westminster Abbey.[32]

MARLAY COURTS EVELEEN

When he began painting Eveleen in 1876 Watts caught her at a very different stage, and it is on this earlier period, before the entrance of Myers on the scene, that we must now concentrate if we are fully to understand the Delaware portrait. Although the sisters were still young, two London seasons had passed since their presentation at Court in May 1874 and yet neither was married. "The Misses Tennant burst upon London as the sensation and glory of the season, but afterwards they hardly kept up to "'the form' of their opening year," one London correspondent observed in 1890.[33] In that "opening year" of 1874–75, the time of the Millais portraits, it had been Dolly who was involved in sentimental coils, but now it was Eveleen who was locked in an impossible relationship. Her suitor was old Etonian Charles Brinsley Marlay (1829–1912) who, like Myers, was a graduate of Trinity College, Cambridge (fig. 6).[34] Marlay was just the sort of husband Gertrude had been seeking for her youngest daughter. He was not only a wealthy landowner, having in 1847 inherited Belvedere House, Co. Westmeath, in Ireland, but better still, given Gertrude's liberal sympathies, a benevolent one, according to the local parish priest, who in March 1880 wrote to the *Westmeath Guardian* that for twenty-five years Marlay had given extensive employment to laborers and tradesmen, built cottages for his tenants, provided a school, and relieved the poor.[35] In London, Marlay lived in a large rented townhouse, St Katharine's Lodge in Regent's Park.[36] At his death he would bequeath his splendid art collection to the University of Cambridge for the Fitzwilliam Museum, together with £80,000 for the enlargement of the museum to accommodate it.[37]

In a curious connection, Marlay had known Millais's wife Effie since early 1851, when she was still married to John Ruskin. In October of that year he met both Ruskins in Venice and spent much time with them.[38] His disapproval of Effie marrying Millais so soon after the annulment of her marriage to Ruskin is recorded in letters to his mother, but until as late as 1873 they both still kept in touch with her.[39] Perhaps he thought to extend his connection with Effie through Eveleen, collecting her, as it were, because she had sat to Millais.

Is there something of Marlay in Henry James's depiction in *The Bostonians* (1886) of Verena Tarrant's suitor Henry Burrage? Verena's friend Olive Chancellor had a theory that Burrage "proposed to almost any girl who was not likely to accept him—did it because he was making a collection of such episodes—a mental album of declarations, blushes, hesitations that just missed imposing themselves as acceptances, quite as he collected enamels and Cremona violins."[40] Verena Tarrant, the daughter of a mesmerist, and a budding medium, also moved, not without peril to herself, among spiritualist circles, as would Eveleen, and their very names resemble each other.

In April 1876 Dolly wrote of Marlay, "I like and shall always like him, he is not so merry as he used to be, even so short a time as last year. Time does sadden people."[41] This suggests the girls had known him since 1875, the year of the success of their Millais portraits at the Academy. Marlay began calling seriously on Eveleen in the summer of 1876, when he was 47 and

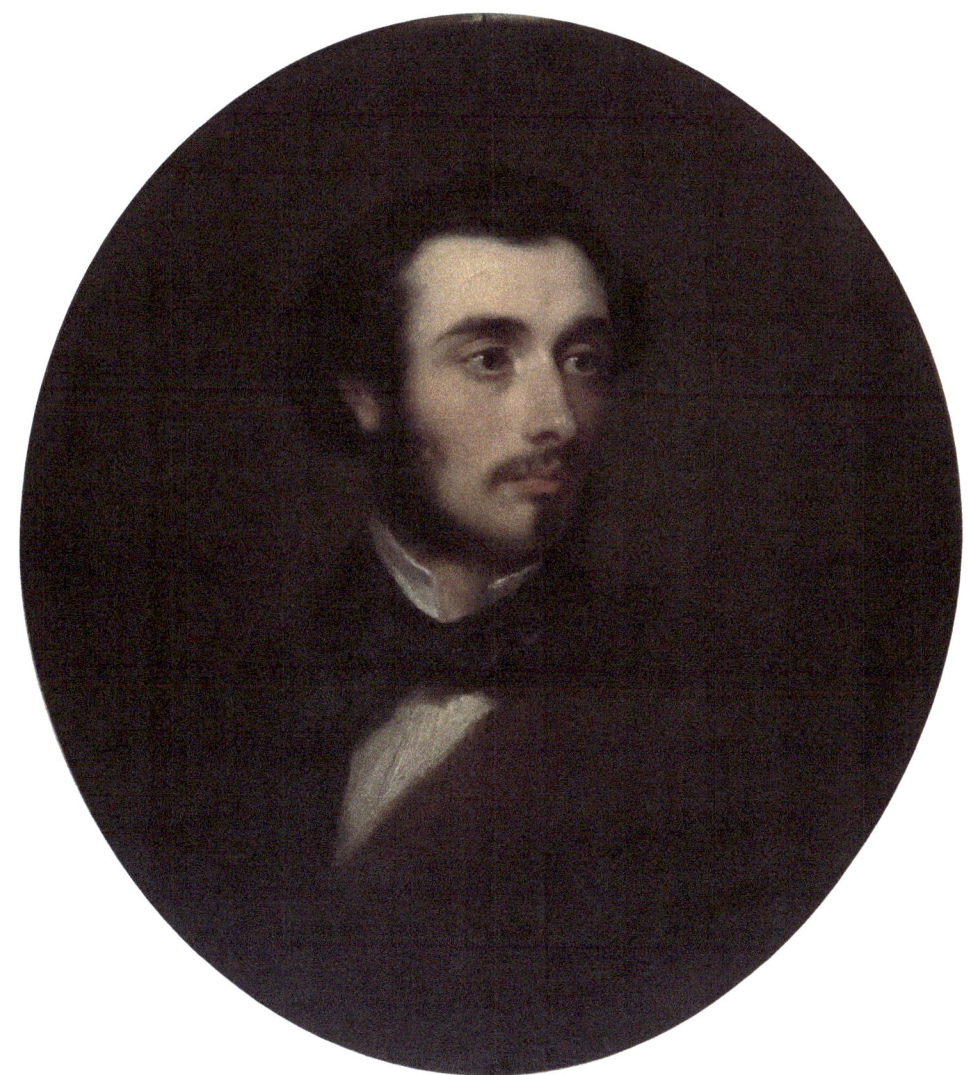

Fig. 6. Artist unknown, probably French, *Charles Brinsley Marlay*, c. 1850, oil on canvas, 673 x 559 mm, © Fitzwilliam Museum, University of Cambridge, M.84

she 19, and invited her and Dolly to a garden party to be held at his house on Friday, July 7. Gertrude, sensing his interest, ordered the girls "such lovely dresses from Elise," society dressmaker Madame Elise being a family friend.[42] Dolly, meanwhile, although she liked Marlay, was protective of her sister and wrote the next day, "I think Mr Marlay admires Eveleen. But he is an Old Man compared to her. And far from strong. I hope he will do no more than admire."[43]

In August he visited them in Trouville, the French coastal resort where in 1842 Gertrude had first met Flaubert, and in Cowes on the Isle of Wight. Dolly wrote later:

> I do not think there is any doubt he much admires Eveleen, but I am not sure that he will ever have the courage to tell her so. Eveleen thinks only of him, and of improving herself, the more to bring herself up to his level. She reads and writes all day long, and has indeed become much more educated. He admires intensely "Lycidas" and when we were at Trouville and he visited Eveleen and Elsie two or three times a day at Cowes, he used to read Shakespeare and Milton. Eveleen now has Lycidas by heart, and through him loves Milton.[44]

On December 16, 1876, in what sounds like a suggestive allusion to the Millais portrait, in which Eveleen was carrying a basket of ferns, Marlay wrote to wrote to Gertrude and enclosed some rare ferns and orchids for Eveleen. His gift caused Eveleen to be "much fluttered" and Dolly to think they were about to lose "dear little Eveleen."[45] On Christmas Day he called and stayed what were to Dolly three long hours as she had to be chaperone, her mother being, perhaps conveniently, ill in bed. Two and a half years later, in July 1879, by which time Eveleen had refused three proposals from others for Marlay's sake, Dolly lost all patience with his procrastination and called him a "selfish foolish man."[46] Gertrude then finally took matters in hand, and tried to force a rupture, writing to Marlay on August 5, 1879, with the return of a sketch by Gustave Doré he had lent to Eveleen: "I must say goodbye to you, in this hurried note, and hope we shall all meet again, sometime or other."[47] Nonetheless, when the Tennants left for Paris on December 5 of that year, Eveleen was still not entirely disentangled from Marlay. The three years of the painting of Watts's Delaware portrait exactly coincide with the duration of their relationship.

WATTS PAINTS EVELEEN

It was in April 1876, after an unsatisfactory affair of Dolly's had run its course and Eveleen's with Marlay not yet begun, that Gertrude seems to have decided to relaunch her daughters on the marriage market. At the end of that month she took them to Paris, the ubiquitous and ever-helpful Hamilton Aïdé acting as chaperone. They called on the most fashionable dressmaker of the day, Charles Frederick Worth, who had established his name by making dresses for the Empress Eugénie.[48] Like an artist arranging sittings for a portrait, he flatteringly gave the girls several fittings and invited the family to his home. Gertrude ordered her daughters black velvet coat dresses with green silk skirts, long white satin embroidered waistcoats and, in the style of G. F. Watts, for it was he whom she next intended to cultivate, velvet skullcaps.[49]

Back in London at the beginning of July, making a statement of their Francophilia in the heart of London, the girls wore their Worth dresses for their big summer garden party at Richmond Terrace and invited both Millais and Watts. With characteristic exuberance they organized both a Hungarian band and a Punch-and-Judy show. "Altogether it was quite a great success, everyone talking of it, the lovely garden, the terrace along the embankment the River beyond, all made it really interesting. —People who cared for Music were quite in raptures about the Band. —and everyone stayed till late."[50]

It is unclear when the Tennants first made the acquaintance of Watts, but it must have been considerably before January 3, 1875, the date of an affectionate surviving letter he wrote to Eveleen.[51] On March 13, 1875, Dolly also hinted at a long preexisting relationship when she wrote in her journal regarding an invitation her mother had sent him to dine at Richmond Terrace: "Mr. Watts, he I once had a decided sentiment for, and who I like much now, is asked."[52] Now, after the success of their garden party, the conditions were ripe for Watts to be reeled in to paint portraits of the Misses Tennant. A plan to spend the previous summer with him had been postponed, and Dolly contacted Watts in late August 1876 to revive the idea. The family would go to Freshwater on the Isle of Wight to be near him and so that Dolly could study his painting technique. Watts wrote welcoming the plan and reminding her, usefully as far as they were concerned, that Eveleen had promised to sit to him.[53] Indeed, he would write on September 17 to his patron Charles Hilditch Rickards that he had come to the Isle of Wight from Harrogate specifically to make a study of "a really beautiful young lady."[54] This was Eveleen. Watts's future wife Mary Fraser Tytler[55] tells us that he was attracted by her "almost southern beauty," a thread that had run though artists' impressions of her since she was a little girl, and one that in 1893 was still central to Myers's description of her:

bird-like gaiety, without a trace of self-consciousness or arrière pensée

something etherial & floating

beauty that knows itself not

the brilliant colouring; the abundant hair worn loosley about the small head & a certain graceful expressiveness of dress; a tone & manner slightly French, foreign, with the Spanish & Oriental air[56]

The girls' brother Charlie was sent ahead to the Isle of Wight to find accommodation. Dolly wrote:

after hunting high and low in Freshwater, he found at last, a most charming large thatched cottage, with garden, kitchen garden, cocks and hens, and actually a pony,—carriage—and a boy to attend to the stable and garden. This sounds very fascinating and rural. Miss Thackeray went there nearly every year. It was there she wrote the "House on the Cliff".—

Best of all we are quite close to Watts, who is only across a field. We are a mile from Freshwater, in the pure real country, nearer Totness bay than Freshwater bay. It sounds as though I should be very happy there.[57]

The cottage was called Fernside. It had a thatched roof and clematis, fuchsia, and vines peeping in at the windows. The family's trunks were delivered by wagon on Tuesday, September 5, and by Thursday Dolly was describing with horror the dark and musty interior of their lodgings, so far from the sweet and peaceful atmosphere of which she had dreamed. The books in the dining room summed up the constricted upbringing of a previous generation of young women. "A glass book case attracted my attention, but it is chiefly furnished with book by Grace Aguilar a bygone writer of moral for young girls. Four or five old volumes of Bow Bells. The *Young Ladies'* Magazine. —A Family Bible, A broken photograph book and hundreds of cheap children's books."[58]

The room intended as her painting room, meanwhile, was "crowded with clumsy china figures, dusty old wool and bead mats, dirty stuffed birds, [and] hideous dried grasses, dyed most unnatural colours."[59] It was not surprising that the girls escaped this oppressive interior as often as they could, running across the field to Watts's contemporary modern space at the Briary, the "unassuming" house "in its setting of great elm trees" that Philip Webb had just completed for him at Freshwater.[60]

I go every morning with Eveleen, to Watts, from ten till a quarter to two. His studio is very large very lofty, and bare, the floor is white deal, the walls whitewashed, the only furniture being his easel, a screen, a high chair, a table with drawers, some shelves and many canvasses of all sizes ranged along the walls. At the further end is a piano and a sofa.[61]

They were constantly at the Briary, to the extent that Gertrude became worried about the suitability of such unchaperoned intimacy with Watts, while typically continuing to let the visits take place.[62] Watts had taken to the girls, however. Mary Watts, who studied sculpture at the Slade from 1872-73 and must have already known Dolly from there, says that the sisters became Watts's "especial friends" and Dolly herself noted that he told them "he looked upon Eveleen and me [...] as his little adopted daughter Blanche."[63]

Eveleen's Tate portrait was begun between September 6 and 10, 1876.[64] Watts first painted her face and hair, but then became stalled for her clothing as he wanted to try out some dresses and materials she had at home in London. On Friday, September 15, Dolly took advantage of this pause in the proceedings to galvanize Watts into making a second, less gloomy portrait of her sister, possibly thinking it would please her mother more than had the first.[65] The high-spirited Dolly did sometimes find Watts's temperament a little melancholy, citing as a rare exception his playfulness

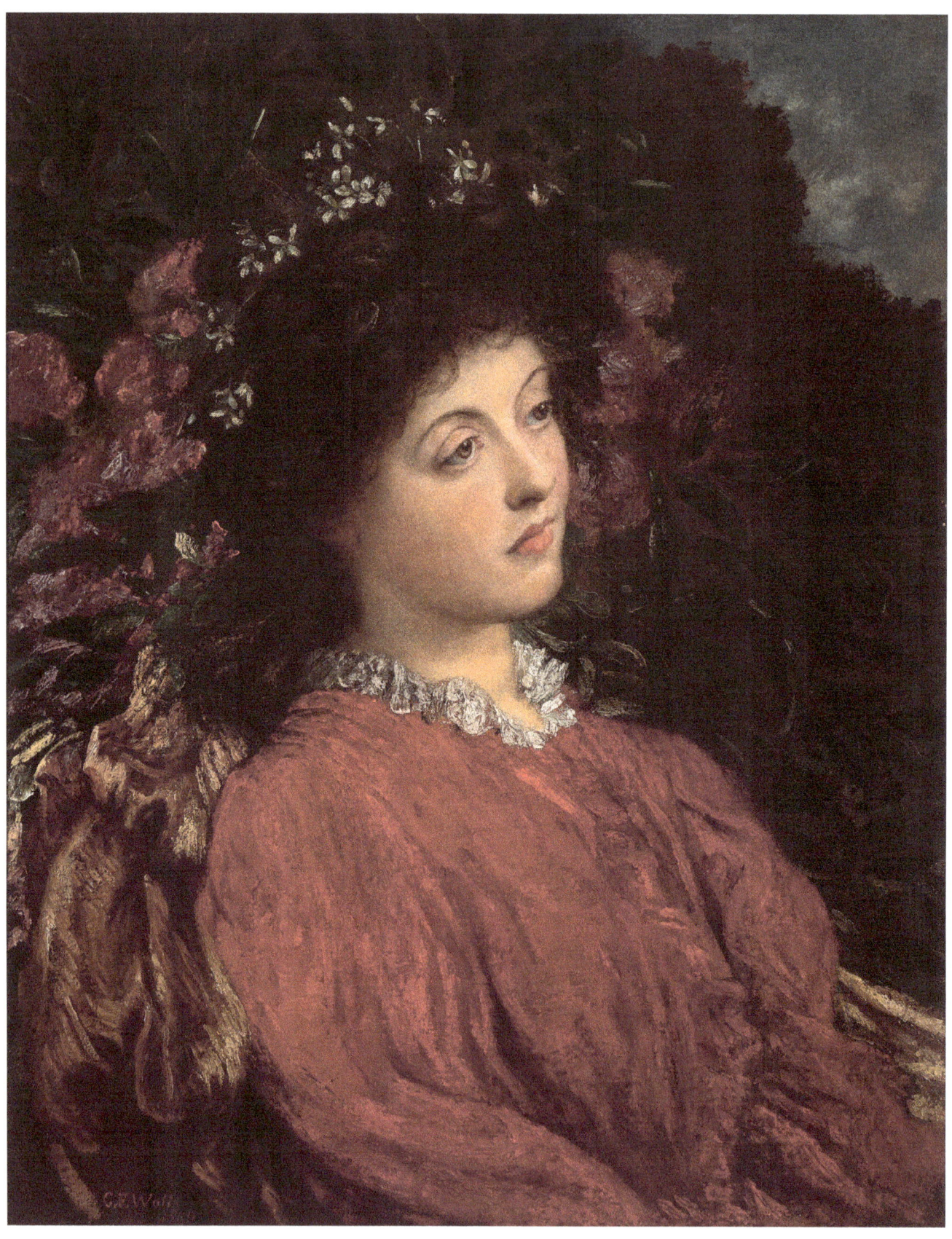

Fig. 7. George Frederic Watts, *Portrait of Eveleen Tennant (Later Mrs. F.W.H. Myers)*, 1876–1879, oil on canvas, 641 x 514 mm, Delaware Art Museum, Samuel and Mary R. Bancroft Memorial, 1935-34

during a trip with Annie Prinsep and Blanche to Alum Bay on September 14, "he was quite cheerful and merry and that he seldom is." Watts showed the party how to throw ducks and drakes, "how to throw up two or three stones at a time and catch them, also how to throw at a mark, but he declared we none of us could 'throw' properly."[66] Seeing him in this lighter mood, Dolly seized her opportunity and the very first thing she did was to displace the frontal pose of Eveleen's previous portraits by Millais and Watts:

> Yesterday Eveleen came up as usual to be painted, but Signor had come to a full stop in his work, he declared he could do nothing more till he had the dress, so he sat listlessly down in an arm chair, and would probably have proposed a walk, but I had an idea, I said, "Signor you <u>shall</u> <u>not</u> go to London tomorrow you will paint another portrait of Eveleen.
>
> I then took her picture off the easel, chose a smaller canvas drew his painting table to the easel, then I made Eveleen sit in an arm chair and throw her head a trifle up and on one side, I ran into the garden to a wall where I recollected to have seen a vine with small green grapes. I pulled off a long trail of green leaves with tendrils and two small bunches of grapes, I returned to Eveleen, arranged the leaves and fruit in her hair, and then drew Signor to the spot where I stood he was much pleased and instantly set to work. I didn't watch behind him all the time as it might have impeded him but I returned to my own work, the children dancing in a ring. I had done it in terra vert so I began to put on the flesh tones [...] We worked hard and silently. At two we ran home together.[67]

The Delaware portrait (fig. 7) was therefore begun on September 15, 1876, just a few days after the first. Eveleen was a good sitter, although on September 16, after she had sat again to Watts, Dolly noted that "Signor would as soon think of insulting one as praising one. He never praises Eveleen, even for her admirable sitting."[68] Dolly records further sittings on October 5 and 7, but the work was abandoned when the Tennants left the Isle of Wight on October 11.[69] Watts now concentrated on Dolly's portrait, which was to be shown at the Academy of 1877. Then, although the girls continued to see Watts, there was, if we follow the evidence of Dolly's journals, a gap of three years before the Delaware portrait was resumed. On October 27, 1879 she wrote that Watts wanted Eveleen to sit to him, as he was "anxious to finish his portrait of her begun at Freshwater, where she is turning round her head, her hair is starred with jessamine and the background is formed of deep red dahlias."[70] On October 30, at the artist's request, the sisters visited him in London, leaving with an appointment for Eveleen to sit on November 4.[71] She sat to Watts for two hours or so on November 11.[72]

On Monday, November 17 the girls "spent a long happy afternoon with him. Eveleen sang—he sang—I read aloud to them the proof sheets of an article he is sending to the 19th Century, on art."[73] As he painted them in the autumn of 1876 Watts had discussed with the sisters the ideas behind this article, "The Present Conditions of Art," which tellingly included passages on dress as well as on "the enigma of being."[74] In the summer of 1879 he was writing it up and published it in the *Nineteenth Century*, at Dolly's urging, the following year. As for the Delaware portrait, he made the finishing touches on Thursday, November 20, 1879. This was, according to Dolly, the last sitting.[75] Myers had resumed his acquaintance with Eveleen six days earlier, on November 14, but neither she nor Watts was aware he intended to begin courting her. On December 5, the Tennants left for Paris and, as we know, Myers followed them.

The Delaware portrait, smaller than the Tate portrait, is more intimate and less imposing but in some ways more of a success. Dolly had reservations, writing on November 22, 1879, "I do like it and think it has a strong resemblance to Eveleen, but she is without flattery so infinitely lovelier than he has painted her. Her face is much more oval, and less broad."76 She added that Watts "thinks of calling it 'Reverie' and will either send it to the Academy or the Grosvenor."77 Although this may have been his intention and the reason for the resumed sittings, in the end he sent it to neither institution and the work by Watts of that name shown at the Grosvenor Gallery in 1881 was of Violet Lindsay, not of Eveleen. Mary Watts, in the manuscript catalogue of Watts's pictures she drew up after his death, in about 1910, gives it the same title as the Tate portrait, *Miss Eveleen Tennant (Mrs F.W.H. Myers)*.78 It was not shown in public until 1885, at the Grosvenor Gallery, and then as *Portrait of Mrs. F. Myers*, in a year when Dolly's paintings *Cupid Disarmed* and *Truth at the Well* shared with it the walls of the West Gallery. Eveleen herself, nine years older now than depicted in the painting and a mother of two, had the public image of her permanently fixed as a nineteen-year-old by this late showing of the work.

Dolly had picked vines to adorn her sister's hair because she was determined to show a more extroverted side of her character than in the rather static earlier portraits by Millais and Watts. Eveleen would, she determined, be a Bacchante (a wild and frenzied female), an interesting choice given Myers's scholarly interest in female hysteria.79 The Bacchantes' cry of frenzy, "Evoë," was even similar to Eveleen's name. Eveleen relished the comparison herself, as her confession to her husband that only to him she could "rush & talk <u>loud</u>'"and be her "wild, natural self" suggests.80 Dolly's account reveals, however, that her desire to have Watts depict Eveleen's passionate nature was attenuated by the artist as the sittings wore on and the portrait began to reflect Watts's character rather than Eveleen's own. She wrote, "Signor's subjects all have a stamp of sadness. Even in his laughing head of Eveleen there is a sad look behind the smile. It is <u>not</u> the head of a Bacchante, but a maiden who has twined vine leaves in her hair, and

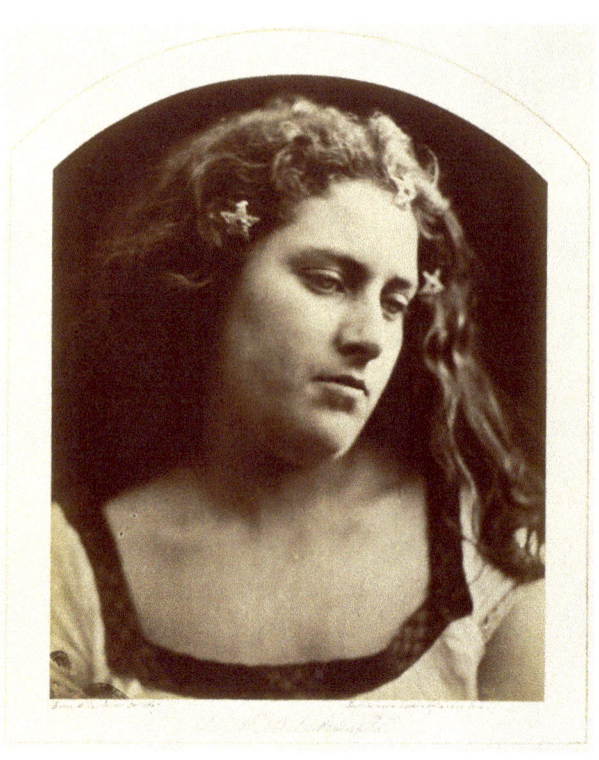

Fig. 8. Julia Margaret Cameron, *[A Bacchante]*, June 20, 1867, albumen silver print, 251 x 200 mm, J. Paul Getty Museum, Los Angeles

is smiling vaguely at thinking herself a Bacchante."80

Dolly's inspiration for Eveleen's portrait may have been Julia Margaret Cameron's photograph, taken nine years earlier at Freshwater, of a markedly unsmiling Cyllena Wilson as a Bacchante (fig. 8). Cameron had given the picture to Watts and inscribed the mount, "For the Signor from Julia Margaret Cameron."82 Watts certainly places Eveleen almost as close to the picture plane as Cameron had Cyllena to the lens, with the same aim of increasing the intensity of the image. Eveleen is said to have owned a number of photographs by Cameron, who had lived on the Isle of Wight since 1860 and only quit Freshwater for Ceylon in 1875.83 The Tennants may have visited her there on family holidays in the 1860s, for Eveleen told an interviewer that it was being photographed by Cameron as a little girl that had inspired her to become a photographer herself.84

When I was a little girl I was taken by my mother to call on Mrs. Cameron, I think the first, and certainly the most famous of artistic photographers. She lived in the Isle of Wight, and her charming home, even apart from her work, was such as to impress the sensitive imagination of a child, the more so that she took a photograph of me enfolded in a blanket and holding a lily, which greatly amused me. The beauty of her work inspired me with a desire of becoming a photographer myself. I even loved the smell of the chemicals [...].[85]

Before Eveleen's sittings for Watts resumed in November, Dolly recalled the picture as she had last seen it, describing Eveleen's hair as starred with jessamine. In utilising jasmine rather than Dolly's original conception of vines, Watts almost immediately diverges from the Bacchante idea. The technical examination of the painting made in April 2021 found "no evidence of an earlier design of grapes and vines in the sitter's hair [...] nor [...] any evidence of the white flowers being changed [...] unless they were thinly applied and do not register on the x-radiograph."[86] What we have here is probably an example of Watts steadily ignoring Dolly's attempts to influence the direction of his picture, as she was wont to do, and quietly working out his own iconography, while placating her by giving the portrait a little of the quality of Cameron's Bacchante, in the sense that Cyllena has stars in her hair. Watts's Eveleen is, however, more of a conventionally marriageable maiden than a Bacchante, jasmine being one of the traditional adornments of the Victorian bride.[87] If it was meant to hint at marriage, however, the hint was meant for Charles Brinsley Marlay, Eveleen's suitor from 1876 to 1879, not Myers. Watts was in effect, for most of the period of the portrait's gestation, painting a marriage picture for Marlay, or even a picture designed to entice him into marriage. He depicts Eveleen as passively waiting, which she did for Marlay but hardly for Myers, whose courtship was rapid in the extreme.

Marlay was known for having created beautiful gardens at both his Irish and his London homes and Watts's portrait does seem designed to appeal to someone with a love of plants.[88] Perhaps Eveleen was even trying to recreate Watts's picture on the occasion in 1878 when, according to Dolly, she bought flowers from Covent Garden, arranged them in pots around her and sat waiting at home for her suitor, "looking so sweetly innocent and lovely."[89] Quite possibly Myers, just before their marriage in 1880, was trying to overlay the image of Marlay and all the bouquets he had bought Eveleen over the years with that of his own largesse in insisting that her wedding bouquet be "really lovely, —as lovely as it can be. I do not say, let it be to other bouquets what you are to other brides, —or it would cost ten thousand pounds, & be too big to go into Westminster Abbey, —but let it be (if that can be) lovelier than any bouquet you have ever had."[90]

In the early years of their married life, Eveleen and Myers were joyous partners in the laying out and planting of their garden at Leckhampton, the house near Cambridge commissioned by Myers in 1878 from his cousin, architect William Marshall.[91] Yet Eveleen, when she wrote to Myers in 1883, suggests that her horticultural knowledge was not only superior to her husband's, but also began before she met him. The two had spent a week with Lady Mount-Temple at Broadlands in Hampshire in October 1880, shortly after their wedding and "how much more you know about gardening than when we were at Broad Lands together," Eveleen remarked.[92] It looks as if it was Marlay who had developed her interest in plants and gardens.

Unaware of the suggestion from Dolly's journals that she and presumably Watts had called the white flowers jessamine or jasmine, Mary Watts, in her catalogue of her husband's pictures, argued vehemently against such an identification and asserted that they were in fact wild clematis or Traveler's Joy.[93] It is true that jasmine has more pointed petals than the flowers in the picture, and five of them, whereas wild clematis has four like the flowers in Eveleen's hair, but Watts would have been hard pressed to find jasmine or wild clematis in flower in autumn. He imagined his flowers, following an artistic plan of his own.

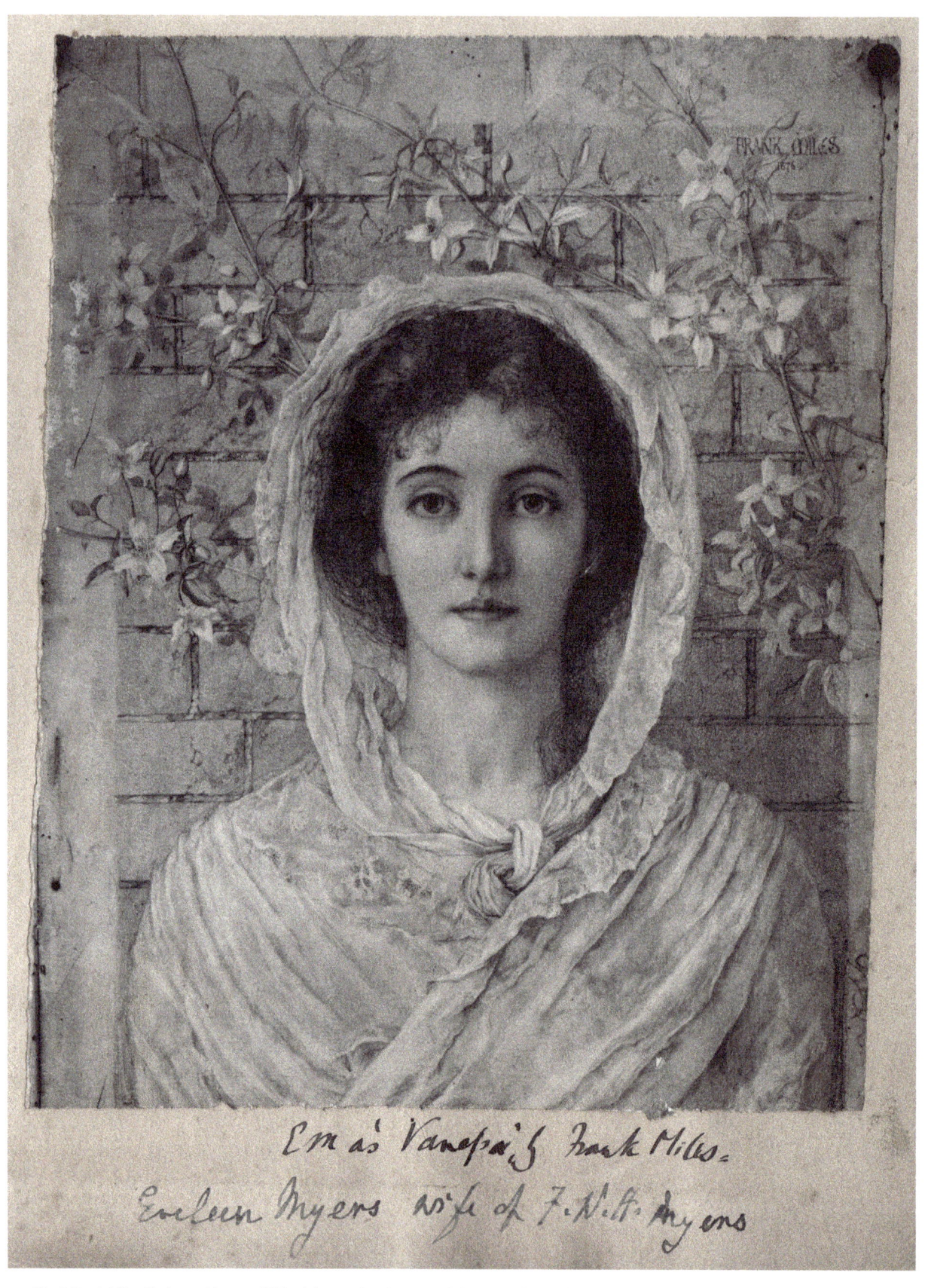

Fig. 9. Frank Miles, *Eveleen as Vanessa*, 1876, platinum print after a pencil drawing, 137 x 110 mm, National Portrait Gallery, London, NPG Ax68345

Part of his thinking seems to have been to create a generalized ideal rather than botanical specifity. The critics who saw the picture at the Grosvenor Gallery in 1885 responded as he probably intended, that is aesthetically, praising the "marvellous wealth of red drapery and green leaves" and the decorative quality of its "rich reds and golden browns and bronze greens."[94] The red flowers, which Dolly in October 1879 had confidently called dahlias, are, like the white ones, too vaguely painted to allow accurate identification, although dahlias could actually have been in flower in autumn.[95] Watts worked more suggestively, however, giving them a passing resemblance to pomegrante flowers, which are symbolic of marriage, and to the camellias of *Choosing* (1864), the portrait of his first wife, Ellen Terry. Whereas Terry is shown straining toward the theatrical showiness of the red blooms, however, Eveleen leans easily among them.[96] Despite its virginal aspect, then, and despite Dolly's reservations, Watts's painting gives a better depiction of Eveleen's passionate nature than the portrait made of her in 1875–76 by Frank Miles, where the clematis flowers behind her are carefully trained against a wall (fig. 9). The clematis in the Watts picture, if clematis it is, is wild. Nonetheless, the deepest and darkest layer of vegetation, behind the virginal white blossom and the red flowers of passion, is laurel, the tree into which the river nymph Daphne was, at her begging, transformed by her father to escape Apollo's attentions. Watts's symbolism is silent but nonetheless penetrating. It is not completely subsumed into a purely aesthetic scheme.

The flowers of Watts's painting take on a further layer of meaning when one recalls that his occasional diminutive for Eveleen was the classicising "Eva" and that he was working on his trilogy of Eve pictures at the time he was painting her.[97] When Dolly visited his London studio on March 20, 1876, he was painting "Eve about to pick the apple," probably *Eve Tempted*, a naked Eve, as opposed to her modestly clothed near-namesake Eveleen, although the similarities are there, both being sensuously absorbed into lush vegetation.[98] On June 22, 1878, Dolly recorded a visit with Eveleen to Watts two days before. "We have not seen him for many months, and by his cordial pleasant manner, I might fancy we were still running in and out of his studio at Freshwater." She noticed "any amount of colossal Eve's about the studio."[99] At the back of Watts's mind when he painted Eveleen were these other Eves, in the Garden of Eden just before the Fall, balanced perilously between the spiritual and material worlds.

Eveleen's future husband certainly thought of her as the archetypal Eve, writing to her on the eve of their marriage, "My darling Evie/ [...] My Eve is leading me into Eden."[100] But his Eve goes further than Watts's. Myers appears to suggest that his modern Eve was powerful enough to reverse the narrative direction of the Genesis story by assuming without guilt the ethical consequences of the Fall. His Eden is less a state of pre-lapsarian innocence than one of unbounded sensualism. In his 1893 autobiography, *Fragments of Inner Life*, Myers, describing the passionate Hellenism of his youth, wrote about traveling to the Greek islands in 1864. "Then it was that Praxilla's cry rang out across the narrow seas, that call to fellowship, reckless and lovely with stirring joy. 'Drink with me!' she cried, 'be young along with me! Love with me! Wear with me the garland crown! Mad be thou with my madness; be wise when I am wise!'"[101] There may be an echo here of the Delaware portrait in the "garland crown."

One can distinguish something of a dialogue between the portraits of Eveleen by Millais and Watts. Both artists suggested Eveleen's sensuality by having the lines of her dress appear to flow into the vegetation around her body. The backgrounds, with their free brushstrokes, also resemble each other. If Millais intended his to be reminiscent of Gainsborough, Mrs. Barrington called the effect in relation to Watts "a free loose touch which gives a palpitating, tremulous quality to the surface of a painting, and approximates, he thinks, nearest to the constant condition of the atmosphere in nature."[102]

Eveleen's dress in Watts's portrait is, of course, red like that in the Millais. Technical analysis tells us more, that its vermilion color, mercuric sulfide, is "painted over a layer of dark yellow ochre-colored paint, presumably to lend a golden tone to the upper layers."[103] The dress is also almost identical to that worn by the seamstress in Watts's *Song of the Shirt* (fig. 10) or *The Seamstress* (c. 1847, Watts Gallery Trust). Given the notoriety attached to the death of one of Madame Elise's seamstresses in 1863, apparently because of poor working conditions, Watts may well, in using this dress or one very like it, have been making a silent commentary on the suffering behind the couture dressmaking to which the otherwise liberal-minded sisters were in thrall, much as Millais had done in *Stitch! Stitch! Stitch!* (1876, Johannesburg Art Gallery).[104]

Millais gave *Stitch! Stitch! Stitch!* to Watts, his successor as the Tennant sisters' portraitist, in July 1876, just before Watts started painting them.[105] Watts hung it in the studio at his London home, Little Holland House "as an example to follow."[106] Millais's picture will have reminded him of the humanitarian sympathies he and his friend shared and which were perhaps at the back of their minds when they painted expensively dressed young women like Dolly and Eveleen. This hypothesis is strengthened by the fact that Watts's *Song of the Shirt* and his Tate portrait of Eveleen were both shown in the 1881–82 Watts show at Grosvenor Gallery, while Millais's *Stitch! Stitch! Stitch!* was lent by Watts to the 1886 Millais exhibition at the Grosvenor and there displayed next to *No!*, Millais's picture of Dolly.

On January 13, 1880, in Paris, a husband, and one she loved, secured, Eveleen wrote a dignified letter to Marlay. Her former suitor, who would never marry, was bewildered by her sudden engagement, but Eveleen's manner was crisp and decided:

> Your letter has touched me more than I can say and under the feelings of deep solemnity with

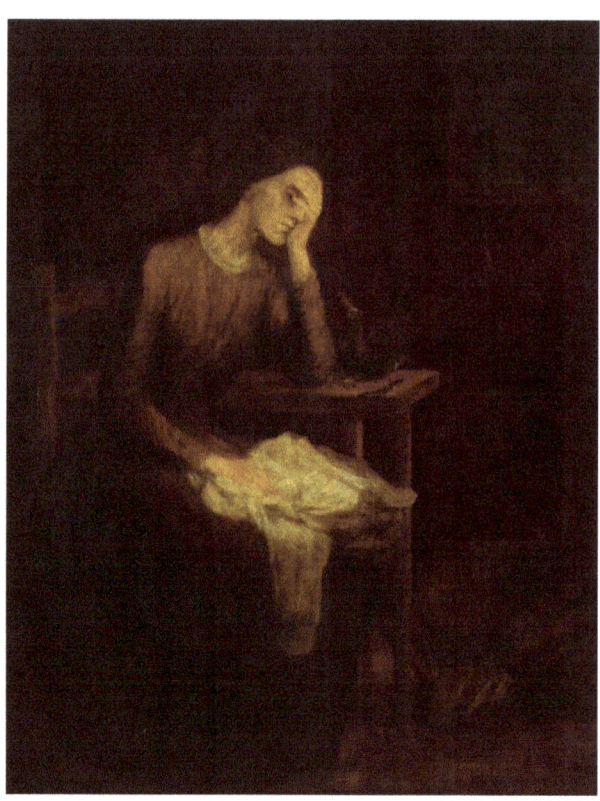

Fig. 10. George Frederic Watts, *Song of the Shirt*, 1850, oil on canvas, 1448 x 1270 mm, Watts Gallery Trust, COMWG 128

> which I feel my maiden life is fast drawing to its close, I venture to break through all established rules, and like a person standing on the brink of another world I will tell you the simple truth. You have played a far greater part in my inward life than you can suppose. When I first knew you I was only just out of childhood, and all the affection I had to give, I gave you. —But the pain I have known has made me better, and wiser, and I am sure you were unconscious of it all. —I can never think of you but with profound regard, and in many ways you have done me good, and fitted me for the life I am soon going to enter on, as the companion of a man of great mental gifts, whose life heretofore has not been happy, and whose home it will be my joy, and duty, to try to brighten.[107]

The expression "inward life" sounds as if it has been acquired from Myers's terminology, as does the phrase "on the brink of another world." Perhaps Myers even dictated the letter to Eveleen. It was, in any event, on this very brink that Watts painted her. The question is whether, if Myers was beginning to influence Eveleen's views, he was not also influencing those of Watts. Could some sense of an "inward life," the radiance of her face perhaps, have been added after his engagement at Myers's behest to reflect how he, the spiritual researcher, foresaw the direction of their marriage?

Myers had been involved in the scientific investigation of what he called the supernormal since the early 1870s, Eveleen's "Millais" period, and his interest had not subsided on his engagement. Indeed, his friend Georgina, Lady Mount-Temple, hostess of the religious conferences held at Broadlands and the high priestess of spiritual investigation; someone, moreover, whose opinion he greatly valued; warned him on January 19, 1880, not to be distracted in the joy of his engagement from the "great pursuit—even in the absorption of present happiness for joy most specially demands Immortality and the Garden of Eden would have no colour or brightness without the sky."[108] One could imagine such a letter impressing Myers deeply and prompting him to follow its precepts by asking Watts to draw out the mystical quality of Eveleen's portrait.

Mary Watts's statement, in her catalogue of her husband's pictures, is ambiguous. Against the Tate portrait she writes: "Miss Eveleen Tennant's […] beauty attracted Mr. Watts to paint two portraits, probably both were begun at the Briary in 1876, but she gave sittings after her engagement in 1880 to Mr. F.W.H. Myers, so well known for his psychical research."[109] It is frustratingly unclear whether Mrs. Watts is referring to alterations made to *both* portraits or just to the Tate one, but if she means both, her dating flies in the face of Dorothy's confident assertion that the Delaware portrait was finished on November 20, 1879.

Before considering the arguments on both sides we must dispense with the misleading evidence of the Delaware portrait being signed and dated "G. F. Watts 1869." This cannot be correct. The evidence of Dolly's journals apart, Eveleen was only thirteen in 1869. Bancroft himself was concerned about the dating, the more particularly because D. Croal Thomson of Agnew's had put "Signed and dated 1862" on the bill of 1900. He asked Thomson to check the date with Mrs. Watts, who replied categorically on June 5, 1906 that "Miss Evelyn Tennant sat for it in 1875 or 6—not 1862."[110] Bancroft reminded Thomson of what he had told him when he first showed him the picture, that "Watts had painted this over thirty years before and had retained it in his Studio until less than a month of the time that I saw it."[111] Taking all the evidence into account, and noting that the picture "has been worked over more than once, and probably more than two or three times," Bancroft concluded that an 1869 picture had been reworked at the Briary in "1875 or 6" with Eveleen as model.[112] We now know, on the evidence of Dolly's journals, that this was not so. Technical analysis categorically states that there is no "7" under the "6" of the date and that both date and signature "appear old and of similar paint quality and handling. Cracks from the lower paint layers extend through the signature and date."[113] This seems to discount any suggestion that Watts, having kept the work by him undated for thirty years, dated it just before selling it, confusing 1869 with 1879. Watts did undoubtedly get his date wrong but it looks as if he must have done so in 1879.

Returning to the question of whether the Delaware portrait was altered after the engagement, we should recall that although Mary Watts first met her future husband in 1870 and visited him at Freshwater in September 1875, she was not there in September 1876 when the picture was begun, nor present in the spring of 1880 when she suggests it was altered. She did not marry Watts until 1886, and so had no firsthand knowledge of the painting's history.[114] She did not, on the other hand, invent her information about sittings taking place after the Myers engagement, but had it directly from Watts.

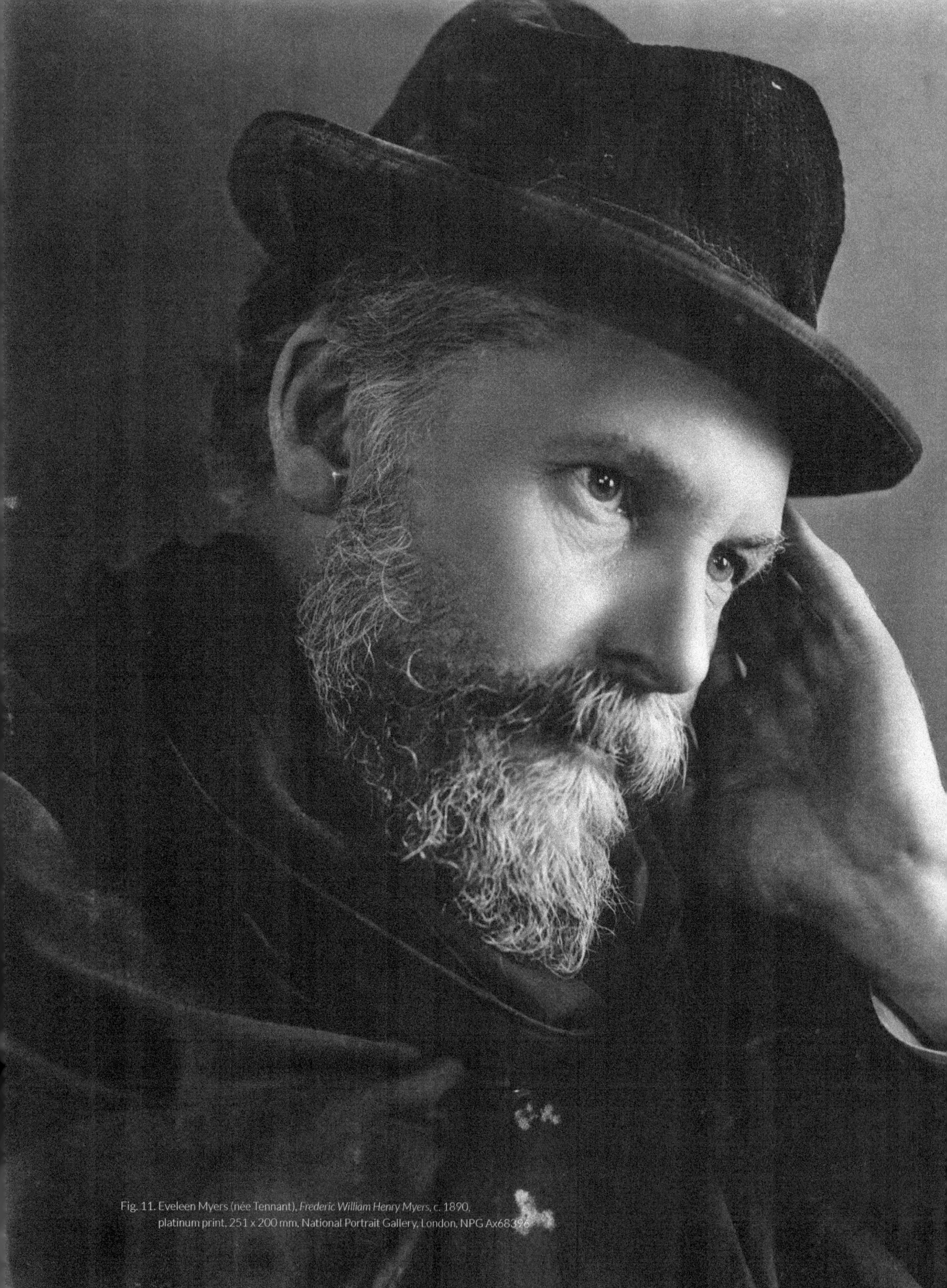

Fig. 11. Eveleen Myers (née Tennant), *Frederic William Henry Myers*, c. 1890, platinum print, 251 x 200 mm, National Portrait Gallery, London, NPG Ax68398.

Could it be that Dolly, who mentions no further alterations after November 20, 1879, was simply unaware that they had taken place?[115]

In fact, between the engagement, which occurred on December 27, 1879, not in 1880 as Mary Watts states, and the marriage on March 15, 1880, there would have been very little time for further sittings. The Tennants remained in Paris until January 31 so that Eveleen could order her trousseau, have her portrait made by Jean-Jacques Henner, and Dolly complete her art studies.[116] Myers spent from December 31, 1879 to January 3, 1880, in England informing his mother and his friend Edmund Gurney of his engagement, but then returned to his fiancée in Paris and stayed there until the nineteenth.[117] The couple had their portraits taken by the Parisian studio Le Jeune to commemorate the engagement. Eveleen, already with a photographer's eye, wrote to Myers, "Your photographs from Le Jeun are splendid, mine are all destroyed because they were not like me, perhaps I may try again."[118] She was starting to prefer to stay in the shadows, urging Fred in London to assume the limelight instead, to "go off and sit for your Photo to Mall & Fox. I should like to see you in all the shop windows in London, if it is a sign, that you are appreciated, & valued by the outside world (as I think it would be)."[119] Nor did she like sitting for Henner, with whom her sister was studying; she did so only because her fiancé requested it and she felt unable to refuse him. "I am going to Henner tomorrow, but I hate it, I do it because you seemed to wish it so much [...]."[120] Perhaps there was an element of maidenly modesty here; she belonged to Myers now and no portrait taker should henceforth ever explore her features so closely as he. She also turned down a request from Carolus-Duran that she sit to him.[121] Now that marriage was assured, she no longer wished to be up for appraisal.

Myers did not mention Eveleen's portraits by Watts in a letter he wrote to Caroline Jebb, the American wife of Cambridge classicist Richard Claverhouse Jebb, on January 21, 1880. In response to Mrs. Jebb's request for information about his fiancée, Myers stated solely that she was the daughter of an MP and man of property and the sister of "a promising artist." The Watts portraits are not mentioned, perhaps because they had at this stage not been exhibited and therefore remained untainted and pure. At this point Myers had not even seen them himself.

The major defining fact he offered Mrs. Jebb was that portraits of both sisters by Millais had hung in the 1875 Academy. Truth compelled him to add, with obvious distaste at his bride's reputation having been sullied by the sale of her image, that "[a]drawing of Frank Miles, entitled Vanessa, and sold in the shops was taken from Eveleen, but I am glad to say is not sufficiently like for anyone to recognise her from it."[122] His fastidiousness is in strict contrast to Eveleen's desire that Myers's photograph be in "all the shop windows."

The Tennants returned from Paris on January 31, 1880, but it was not until March 8 that Watts wrote proposing to see Eveleen.[123] Sincerely wishing her happiness, he accounted for his silence by explaining that he had been ill.[124] On the following day, March 9, losing no further time, Myers and Eveleen visited him, Myers noting in his diary: "E & clocks with Arthur, & at Watts. portrait of her. Cold bad."[125] The first and most important point to extract from this brief note is that Myers only refers to seeing a portrait at Watts's studio, not portraits. Of the two, it is far more likely to have been the Tate portrait that Watts had on show, for this was the one that was to be shown at the Royal Academy shortly after the marriage to make a public advertisement of Eveleen's new status. This minute piece of evidence, this omitted "s," is vital because it suggests that it was only to the Tate portrait that alterations were made. We may infer from it that Watts, despite having previously intended, as he had told Dolly, to show the more intimate Delaware portrait at the Academy or the Grosvenor, changed his mind after hearing of the engagement and on March 9 withheld it from Myers.

The second point to take from the note is the improbability of this visit to Watts's studio, a mere six days before the wedding, when Myers was cold-ridden, having involved a sitting. While it is understandable that Myers might have been concerned to give a slightly different connotation to a portrait begun when Eveleen was still in love with Marlay, it is easier to imagine this addition having been the butterfly brooch at Eveleen's throat in the Tate portrait. No formal sitting would have been required for this, and a butterfly, emblematic of Psyche and of the soul, is just the sort of change a classicist and spiritual researcher like Myers might have proposed. Perhaps then, this is all to which Mary Watts was referring when she wrote of changes made to the pictures between the engagement and the marriage. The recent technical analysis of the picture has found no evidence of major design changes by the artist after its original painting.[126] With this the balance tips heavily in favor of Dolly's rather than of Mary Watts's evidence and to a dating of 1876–79 for the Delaware portrait.

The striking radiance of Eveleen's face is thus less likely to have been given to her on a hint from Myers than by Watts himself. It was a quality inherent in her before Myers began to instruct her in spiritual matters, and Watts who perceived it. In 1880 Marlay, writing to Gertrude after she had told him of Eveleen's engagement, alluded to her "charms of person & of mind."[127] In 1937 her *Times* obituarist described the "charm," again, "made vivid by her unusual vitality, which she had the gift of imparting to others, so that even in her advanced years to be in her company was to experience an enhancement of life."[128] Watts penetrated her character more deeply than either of these observers, probing beneath the surface to reveal a child in transition to adulthood, her face radiant with the brightness of youth or of all that she hoped to bring to a husband perhaps, but above all of her own clearsightedness. The glimpse of sky is strangely sunless and the source of light seems to be Eveleen herself. Technical analysis reveals that Watts achieved this radiance by using for the face an extremely dense patch of white lead paint over his favorite bright yellow oil ground and by building up the paint into a smoother surface than the rest of the design.[129] Watts does not, however, imply that the light in Eveleen's face is a spiritual one and, despite what we know retrospectively about Myers, nor should we.

MYERS PURSUES WATTS

The question of why Watts seems to have kept the Delaware portrait to himself on March 9 can only really be answered by examining the relationship between him and Myers. Myers undoubtedly had Wattsian aspirations, as a comparison between the photograph of him taken by Eveleen (fig. 11) with Watts's self-portrait (fig. 12), makes clear but it is less clear that Watts reciprocated them. He was one of the first people Eveleen wrote to from Paris about her engagement. In his reply he assured her that she had made a wise choice, meaning, presumably, in choosing Myers over Marlay.[130] This was far from being a full endorsement of Myers and subsequent events suggest that while Myers made every effort to cultivate Watts, the artist himself kept some distance. Even Mary Watts, in her three volume biography of her husband, *George Frederic Watts: The Annals of an Artist's Life*, despite often mentioning Myers, never calls him her husband's friend.[131] We should be wary of using Myers's statements about the nature of their relationship to reflect both sides of the story.

The Grosvenor Gallery retrospective of Watts's work, which included Eveleen's Tate portrait but not the Delaware one, ran from December 31, 1881 to March 31, 1882. It was therefore in full spate on February 20, 1882, the date of the founding of the Society for Psychical Research (SPR), with which Myers was deeply involved, and the two events must have been intertwined in his mind. Having visited the Grosvenor exhibition with Eveleen on January 6 and then alone on the ninth, Myers wrote to Watts to

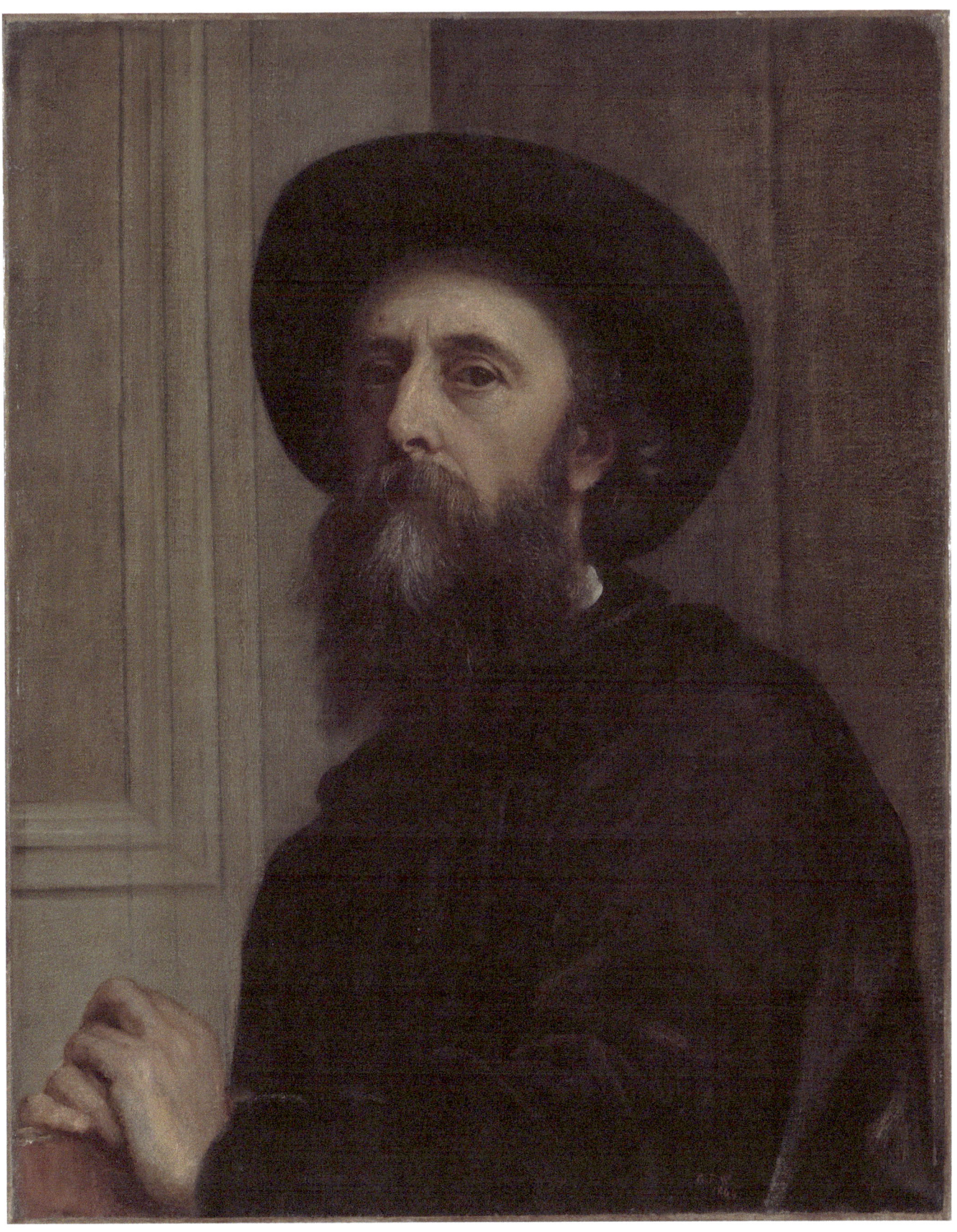

Fig. 12. George Frederic Watts, *Self-Portrait*, 1864, oil on canvas, 648 x 521 mm, Tate, London, N01561

ask if the Tate portrait could be his. We are possibly seeing here an example, as his attitude to the Millais portrait had been, of Myers wishing to possess an object in order to use it for thought transference.[132] Watts may have suspected this himself, but not to be cajoled by what Caroline Jebb in 1878 called Myers's "insidious nature," he kindly but firmly refused the request.[133] "I have as you know built at great expense a Gallery at Little Holland House. The portrait forms in my opinion one of its chief ornaments & I think at the present I can hardly spare it."[134]

He did offer Myers first refusal should he ever decide to part with the picture, but in fact, although the contents of the Little Holland House Gallery, where it hung, were in 1903 transferred to his new gallery at Compton in Surrey, Watts kept the Tate portrait until his death in 1904. It could well have been the same impulse that led him to keep the Delaware portrait from Myers on March 9, as if he would not allow Eveleen's image to be entangled in Myers's researches. It would remain under his protection, if the subject herself could not.

In contrast to his complete lack of public response to the Millais exhibition at the Fine Art Society in 1881, Myers was enthusiastic and visible with regard to the Watts retrospective, publishing in February 1882 a poem in the *Fortnightly Review* entitled "Stanzas on Mr Watts' Collected Works."[135] Eveleen herself, probably at her husband's request, wrote to Watts to inform him of its imminent appearance. His reply, which she preserved, seems on the face of it purely self-deprecating but may conceal a slight edge. "I must say how much it gratified me to find that any efforts of mine can by the Poet be felt of sufficient importance to be glorified by poetry."[136] Far from succumbing to Myers's blandishments, Watts sounds as if he suspects that Myers was engaging in self-publicity under the guise of glorifying the artist, and building on his wife's connection with him to enhance his poetic and social reputation. He may not have realized this aspect of things quite yet, but Myers was probably already launching a campaign to enlist his support for the SPR, one in which he succeeded in March 1884 when Watts agreed to become an honorary associate member.[137] Roger Luckhurst has called the SPR's maneuvres to ally itself with famous men "a blatant attempt to install an elite hegemony to counter emergent scientific groups."[138] Eveleen's connection with Watts was, for Myers, vital to this campaign.

Watts's conception of spiritual phenomena, as the portraits were being painted, was certainly at a very different level from that of Myers's research. He did not seek to explain them, while Myers abundantly did. One evening in September 1876 at Freshwater, for example, after singing duets with Eveleen, Watts related to the party his experiences of spirit visitation, one of a figure leaning over him at night at Little Holland House and another of a winged creature flying around his studio whispering "Anima mia, anima mia." "When we went home it was dark and Eveleen kept tightly up to me and Charlie," Dolly noted. She paid tribute to Watts's sincerity, "Signor's evidence is indubitable, he is not a man who would invent or even embroider a story."[139] This story of the winged soul is, however, also recounted by Mary Watts in her life of her husband, and there it is prefaced by a passage that acts as a brake on any tendency to exaggerate Watts's belief in an unseen or spirit world.[140] "Of any psychical faculty he was not in the least conscious, he never encouraged anything of the sort in himself by going to séances or making acquaintance with mediums. Strange things happened to him, he knew, but how they occurred, or what they meant, he did not attempt to explain."[141]

Not long afterward, indeed, on December 2, 1876, Watts was evidently so little convinced of the existence of a spirit afterlife that he took the Tennant girls and Blanche to see the magicians John Neville Maskelyne and George Cooke at the Egyptian Hall, Piccadilly, a place described as "a haven for antispiritualists."[142] As a practicing magician, Maskelyne was sceptical about the existence of the supernatural and had already been critical of Eveleen's future husband's credulousness, as he saw it, in that regard. He would become more so.[143] Rather unexpectedly, on July 12, 1880, Myers, who had privately broached the subject of spirits with Eveleen, also took her to see Maskeleyne, but his only comment on the occasion was that Eveleen was "exquisite."[144] He evidently spent more time looking at her than at Maskelyne and one suspects the outing was at her suggestion rather than his.

The portraits were begun at a time when the only psychical phenomena by which we know Eveleen to have been moved were the stories told her by Watts, but finished just before she married one of the foremost spiritual investigators in the country. This extraordinary transition inevitably caused some comment in her circle. In October 1876 Dolly showed how at ease she was with the sympathies of that circle by introducing Watts to her friend Thomas Henry Huxley, the Darwinian scientist. Myers, although he records in his diary a speculative interest in Huxley's daughter Marian in 1878–79, was an outsider to this group.[145] In February 1880, after the engagement, Dolly confessed in her journal to mixed feelings about her sister's choice, "Fred I know is high minded—spiritual—good—but oh—I would for my part rather die than have been his wife."[146] She went on to speak with regret to Huxley of Myers's interest in spiritualism. Huxley, who had little time for such matters, "looked supremely contemptuous and said it was indeed regrettable."[147] He added, with a possible allusion to the studies being made into female hysteria by French neurologist Jean-Martin Charcot, "I should think that your sister is of such a disposition highly nervous & emotional—it can be seen merely in the way she moves I could make her—or she could be made—without any difficult[y] a most powerful medium. Mr Myers should beware of mixing your sister up in spiritualism. If he can keep his head—well & good—but with a woman you can answer for nothing."[148]

In fact Huxley's comment reflected the prevailing male assumption that women were more fragile than men, a view certainly not shared by Myers, who had since the late 1860s been actively involved in the promotion of higher education for women.[149] Huxley was not being quite fair to Myers, a serious and highly intelligent man who was genuinely perplexed by Huxley's determined subsequent opposition to his work.[150] He seems to have believed that its systematic, scientific nature and the fact that he was undertaking it, as he believed, for the benefit of mankind, might legitimately have won him over. In a review of Darwin's *Life and Letters* (1887) entitled "Charles Darwin and Agnosticism," for example, Myers made plain that he accepted evolution as a fact and wrote with admiration of Huxley's "trenchant polemic" with the sole reservation that it had "cast a kind of glory about the mere fact of man's ignorance which cannot possibly be kept up for long."[151] It was thus with sadness that in his draft autobiography of 1891 he was obliged to cite Huxley as one of those most opposed to the work of the SPR.[152]

Huxley, however, was not completely off the mark in his fears for Eveleen, for Myers, whose 1878 diary contains entries stating that he had mesmerized "MR" and "BT," also, early in his marriage, experimented with mesmerising his wife.[153] She told the spiritualist magazine *Light* in 1934:

> Once in very early days, my husband made the experiment of trying to hypnotise me. After some passes he suggested that I couldn't open my eyes. I attempted to do so and failed. Rather frightened, I stood up before a mirror in a vain effort to see myself, and tried with all my might, and with the help of my hands, to open my eyes. But still I found it impossible. From that day on I had no difficulty in believing in the reality of mesmerism or hypnotism.[154]

Eveleen also tried, privately, to act as a medium after Myers's death in order to communicate with her husband, typically wishing to use her own powers or vision to do so rather than the intermediary of others.[155] Yet Huxley was not being entirely fair to her either, for in the same 1934 interview, sounding utterly in command of the situation, she suggests that she had always been more skeptical of fraudulent mediums than her husband. Her first phrase could, incidentally, equally apply to her experience in sitting to Watts:

> I believe that as a sitter I am naturally a good subject; I mean that through me a connection seems to be easily established with the unseen world. But, on the other hand, I am very much on my guard against giving mediums information unawares; and my standard of what constitutes good evidence is very high; I am not quick to be impressed by results which some others might consider remarkable.[156]

Her qualities of clear thinking and clear seeing were unsuspected by Huxley and possibly also by Dolly, but they were, to his credit, precisely those that Myers admired in her. Shortly after their engagement Eveleen had written to him with remarkable insight for a twenty-three-year-old addressing a man thirteen years her senior, "I sometimes am glad you are a true poet, & then at others I fear you are wanting in common sense."[157] He in turn wrote to her in the early months of their marriage, "I do so value your candour of mind [...]. You have been born with clearer vision, and endowed as it were with an individual revelation [...]. Ah, what a comrade [...]."[158]

There would, however, be a crisis in their marriage in 1884. Eveleen was then housebound with two young children, her concentration on whom left her husband feeling excluded. She in turn was hurt by the frequency with which he was absent, not only in his work as Inspector of Schools for Cambridge district but, increasingly, on SPR business. Although she broadly sympathized with the aims of the SPR, she failed to understand how attempting to prove the existence of a future spirit life could take precedence over present happiness. "I love you better than all the Universe" is a frequent, poignant lament in her letters to him. In a long, sometimes hectoring letter of October 11, Myers told her that in psychical research he had found his vocation; now all he asked was that she assume hers by accompanying him in his quest, "that you may grow in height & width in these years that remain to us together so far as to leave you on quite a different level from that most girlish innocent wh. I first knew; —a rise wh. will retain all the innocence, & add the wisdom & the salvation."[159]

Eveleen, perhaps to his relief, took this well enough and two days later Myers built on the advantage gained with a shaft against her family:

> My Darling Wifie
>
> What a dear little letter from you this morning! I was afraid you might think that my last epistle was rather a sermon! [...] Don't mind what your dear people say or think about these matters:—they look at the universe thru a rather small peephole.[160]

Eveleen tried to read the books he had prescribed for her improvement but struggled. "I like the books you so kindly got me. I have been reading some rather spiritual ones [...]. I hope I may gain light and wisdom from them."[161] Dutifully, however, she gave the SPR £5 from her own money and earned from Myers the accolade, "You never spent any money in a way which gave me so much pleasure!"[162]

When Dolly and Gertrude went to stay with Eveleen at Leckhampton in December 1884, things had obviously not much improved. Dolly wrote in her journal:

> I wish dear Eveleen's life were less isolated. Fred is so much given up to his Psychical research when not engaged with school inspection that Eveleen has none of his companionship the little granted, is given watch in hand I suppose allowances are due

seeing he is "on higher thoughts intent" but the humble & home joys of loving companionship, the house of happy idle talk the <u>being</u> together this is not given to Eveleen—and Leo is her only and most adored companion, but such close and unique fellowship is not good for either, Eveleen must be three years old with him, or he risks guessing at the sadnesses & preoccupations of maturity.[163]

There is no doubt that Eveleen sounded much more lively the following March when she was let off the leash to enjoy the social life of Richmond Terrace.[164]

Some thirty years after Myers's death, in the interview for *Light*, Eveleen defined the difference between her husband and herself as consisting in the fact that her Christian faith had never wavered, whereas Myers, the son of an Anglican clergyman, had lost his in 1869, the year he resigned his Trinity Fellowship. Eveleen did not see this as a serious breach between them, preferring to dwell on the social, philanthropic nature of her husband's work, which had more in common with her own family's interests.[165] She argued that as a result of his research into the survival of the spirit Myers had "brought faith to so many who have needed this support."[166] Myers himself claimed that his work provided evidence that would ultimately prove the truth of the Resurrection, that would in other words restore him to harmony with his wife's religious beliefs.[167] He described himself in his autobiography as "a man of sensuous and emotional temperament, urged and driven by his own personal passion into undertaking a scientific enterprise, which aims at the common weal of men."[168] This is a gloss on his research which must in part have appealed to Eveleen, even if her discovery of the nature of that personal passion, the extent of his obsession with Annie Marshall, ultimately made her miserable.[169] In her commonplace book, in a note apparently made after Myers's death, she composed her own epitaph. It makes clear the extent of her desolation.

She loved much.
She suffered much.
And <u>now</u> she knows
The reason why.[170]

Before turning to the purchase by Bancroft of Eveleen's portrait we should bid farewell to Watts. As Dolly's interests gradually turned more to politics than to art she found it hard to keep in touch with the artist of whom she had been so fond. He lamented in a postscript to a letter to Eveleen of February 1882, "What is become of Dolly? I have not seen her for about a year, & am apparently forgotten."[171] When he went to Cambridge on June 13, 1883, to receive an honorary Doctor of Laws degree, he called to have tea with Eveleen and her infant son Leo at Leckhampton.[172] Immediately afterward Eveleen rushed to tell Dolly all about it. Her letter, which Dolly pasted into her journal, reproaches her for neglecting her old mentor.

> Dearest Dolly
> Watts has just been here he was so enraptured with the whole visit, he thought the house so exquisite & Leo & the garden—he sat in the cool drawing room with the hose playing just outside, & had a delicious tea
> [...]
> He rushed here he told me directly after lunch, He was so <u>loving</u>, so admiring, so enchanted, he wants to come to stay, he said he had no idea! my home was like this, it was the happiest part of his day.
> Please forgive scrawl to catch post & wich in the flash of the moment I know you will like to hear! He admires <u>you</u> so <u>tremendously</u>. He thinks no one like you. He says if I will get you he will come to stay when ever you will –
> EM [173]

In November 1883 Myers asked Eveleen and Dolly to vote for whom they considered to be the finest contemporary portrait painters, noting the results in his diary: Millais first, then Watts and Frank Holl.[174] In 1888 he asked them more specifically to name the six best. Perhaps influenced by their years of knowing Myers, for whom Watts was the ideal painter, they now put Watts at the head of the list, followed by Lawrence Alma-Tadema, Edward Burne-Jones, William Quiller Orchardson, and Holl, with Millais, the painter of likeness, only added in pencil at the end.[175] It is hard to imagine the sisters relegating Millais to an afterthought; it is more conceivable that Myers, their scribe, should have done so.

Although Myers died in 1901 at fifty-seven, three years before Watts, he visited the painter in his old age, as he described in his manuscript draft autobiography of 1893. "Mr Watts was another sympathiser of the truest type. Sitting in his studio with that lofty-minded old man, the true type of an artist, I have drawn high hope from his serene spirituality."[176] In the version of *Fragments of Inner Life* privately printed for his wife and friends the same year this passage does not appear and Watts is merely allied to the names of Tennyson and Ruskin as one of the "elder men" who had shown him "encouraging kindness."[177] In further proof sheets of 1900, Watts is grouped with a different pair, Gladstone and John Couch Adams, as "sympathisers of the truest type," nothing more.[178] When Eveleen had full control, in *Fragments of Prose and Poetry*, the version of her husband's autobiography she edited with four of her photographic portraits and published in 1904, there were no references to Watts at all, although she did reprint in the same volume "G. F. Watts, R. A." This short piece by Myers, "written shortly after visiting Watts some years ago," had just been published in the *SPR Journal* on the occasion of Watts's death. In it Myers quoted Watts as having told him in his last years that the world of the "sacred symbol" was all he had ever really cared about or tried to express. "When I last saw Mr. Watts, in great old age, among the symbolic pictures of his later years, he seemed to me to have become himself a sacred symbol; and I should scarcely have wondered, as I gazed on him, if he had vanished into air."[179]

This, his poem of 1882, "Stanzas on Mr. Watts' Collected Works," aside, is Myers's most fulsome assessment in print of Watts. In "Autobiographical Fragment," the version of his autobiography edited by Eveleen and published at the head of Myers's *Collected Poems* in 1921, there was, again, no reference to the painter. One has the impression that Eveleen, after her husband's death, tried to moderate her husband's overheated assessment of his closeness to Watts and indeed of Watts's to the SPR. She knew the artist very well and doubtless understood him on a human level better than did her husband.

It would be unfair to conclude, however, without mention of a letter Eveleen wrote to her husband in June 1899, which suggests that it was in fact Myers who neglected Watts, his mind being set firmly on the afterlife while his wife was left to cultivate their human contacts. "Darling I had a touching visit to dear Watts. He longs to <u>see you</u> Dolly's only free dates are 10th-11-12-17th. Watts spoke of <u>you</u> with such <u>admiration.</u> He is very <u>noble</u> & good like you que je <u>T'aime</u>."[180]

BANCROFT ACQUIRES EVELEEN

Apart from exhibiting it at the Grosvenor Gallery in 1885 and at the Autumn Exhibition of the Corporation of Manchester Art Gallery in 1897 (cat no 209), where it was listed as "not for sale," Watts kept the Delaware portrait of Eveleen close at hand until 1900. When, in May that year, he did decide to sell, it went to Agnew's, the Manchester and London dealers. On October 25, 1900, Samuel J. Bancroft Jr. bought it there during a trip to London with his wife.[181] The price, inclusive of freight and duty, was £1,275 6s, or about $6,200.[182] Eveleen's portrait by Watts thus traveled to the United States as the earlier Tate portrait had done fifteen years previously, when it was lent to the Metropolitan Museum of Art in New York for the Watts retrospective of 1884–85.[183] The Delaware portrait, however, formed part of a different historical

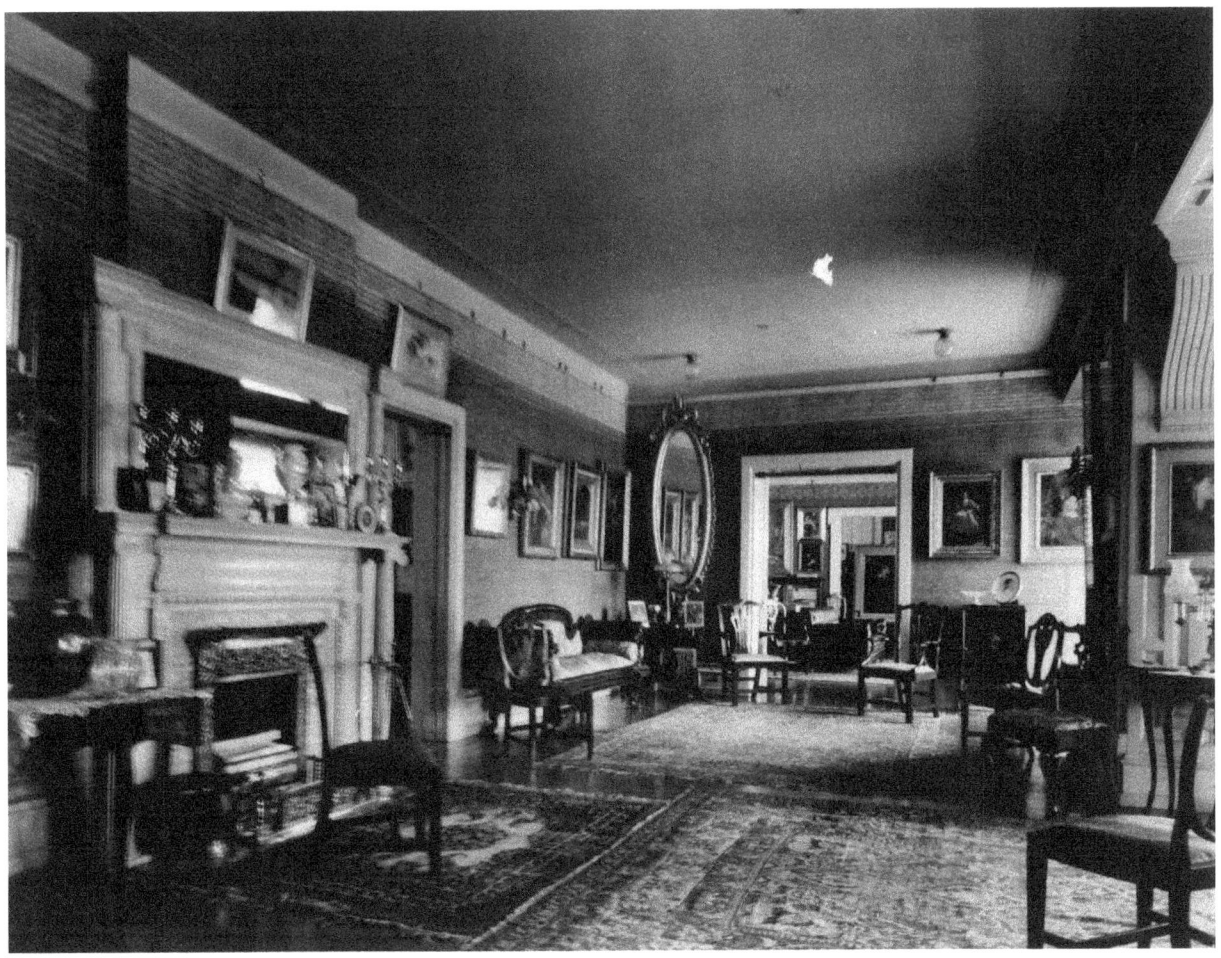

Fig. 13. Edward Bringhurst, *Drawing Room in Rockford, Home of Samuel Bancroft Jr.*, 1937, photographic print, Delaware Art Museum, Samuel and Mary R. Bancroft Pre-Raphaelite Manuscript Collection. Watts's portrait of Eveleen is on the back wall, second to the right of the doorway, next to Millais's *White Cockade*.

movement, that of the torrent of European works of art being bought up at the turn of the century by American collectors. Henry James, who was fond of Eveleen, lamented the trend in his final novel, *The Outcry* (1911). Myers would also have regretted the loss of his wife's portrait for a price and to a stranger, although he might have managed to give its crossing the threshold into the New World a spiritual significance, having in *Fragments of Inner Life* (1893) used Europeans' arrival in the Americas as a metaphor for the investigation of the supernormal. "A new discovery is needed, —to be made by no single Columbus, but by the whole strain of humanity; by the devotion of a world-wide labour to the deciphering of that open secret which has baffled the too hasty or too self-centred wonder and wish of men."[184] Frankly, though, the picture made its journey across the Atlantic thanks to the solid wealth and purchasing power of the material world. Even Eveleen came rather to revel in that fact, crowing to a reporter in 1933 that "there are pictures of me all over the world."[185]

In 1906 Bancroft wrote to Agnew's David Croal Thomson to try to clear up the uncertainty regarding the dating of the picture. He reminded him of the history of the purchase: "You had been trying to buy it at several times but [...] Watts was disinclined to sell it, but [...] at your last visit to him you found that Lady Watts was very anxious to have certain monies put into one of her pet charities and had persuaded her husband to sell this [...]."[186] Thomson wrote to Mary Watts, who in her reply made a separate, rather pointed observation, "I was puzzled by your question about the picture called "Jessamine," for I never heard it so called. Possibly Mr. Watts suggested this title—did he? Or has it taken it to itself since then?"[187] Rowland Elzea has also argued that it was Agnew's that gave the picture the title *Jessamine*, possibly with the aim of making it appear a more saleable subject painting.[188] This suggestion seems to be borne out by the fact that Agnew's Picture Stock Book for 1900 lists it as *Mrs. Fred. Myers (Jessamine)*, whereas it was shown at the Grosvenor Gallery in 1885 as *Portrait of Mrs. F. Myers*.[189] Dolly, however, had used "jessamine" to describe the jasmine flowers in the picture as far back as 1879, which suggests that the slightly archaic word came from her and the artist and that the dealers' title did indeed emanate from Watts.[190]

Bancroft told Gerald Agnew in a letter of April 6, 1909, that he had first hung the portrait in the drawing room at Rockford, his home in Wilmington (fig. 13), next to Edith Martineau's watercolor *In Sweet Music*, which he bought in 1893.[191] Later he substituted for the Martineau a 1908 purchase, one of Millais's Jacobite pictures entitled *The White Cockade* (1862, fig. 14).[192] By coincidence, Millais had originally intended his portrait of Eveleen to be a Jacobite picture.[193]

Bancroft placed Eveleen's portrait in the drawing room, rather than in the more masculine "den" he added to his home in 1892 to enjoy a more intense dialogue with certain of his acquisitions.[194] Dante Gabriel Rossetti's *Found*, for example, with its subject of prostitution, took pride of place in the den. It was in Bancroft's drawing room, however, that the intimate portrait of Eveleen was seen for the first time since 1885 by a wider audience, and took the step toward exposure to the general public that it now enjoys in the Delaware Art Museum.[195]

After completing the portrait, Watts, in contrast, had withdrawn it into a private realm, possibly, as Thomson suggested to Bancroft, his studio.[196] It did not, unlike the more theatrical Tate portrait, form part of the gallery at Little Holland House, appearing

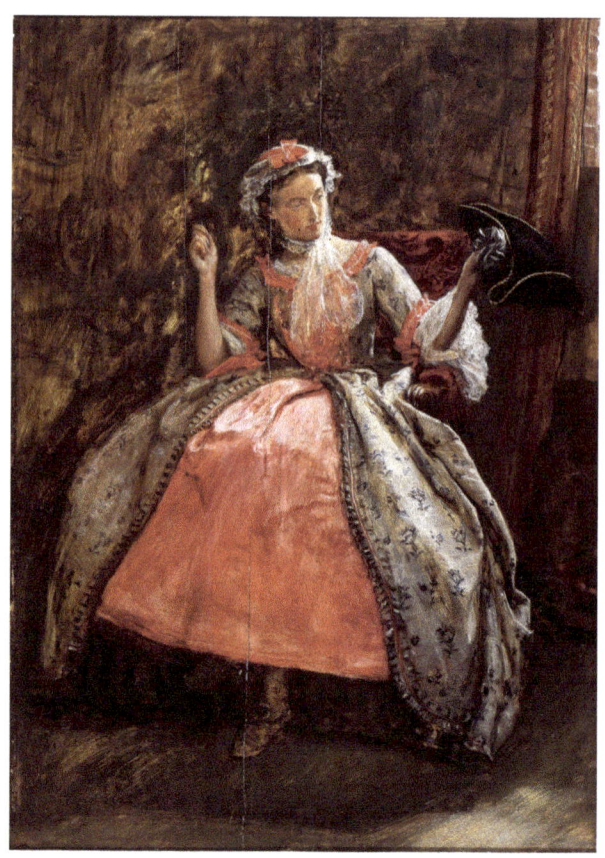

Fig. 14. John Everett Millais, *The White Cockade*, 1862, oil on panel, 567 x 432 mm, Delaware Art Museum, Samuel and Mary Bancroft Memorial, 1935-14

in none of the photographs of that public space. Thomson told Bancroft that it "was painted for the Watts' own home & he had it beside him for many years."[197] Frederick Hollyer, who photographed it, told Thomson that it was "a favorite picture with Watts" and wondered that he had been willing to part with it at all.[198] The fact that it had only rarely been tainted by public view, an aspect Thomson was of course emphasizing to Bancroft to increase its desirability as a purchase, would have appealed to a private collector like Bancroft, who was in a sense buying a virgin. There is something virginal too about the appearance of the work, deriving from Eveleen's high Quakerish collar (Bancroft was a Quaker) and childlike expression. It is, on the face of it, strongly at variance with a picture that *did* hang in the drawing room with Eveleen's portrait: Bancroft's 1892 purchase of Rossetti's *Lady Lilith* (1866-88, fig. 15).

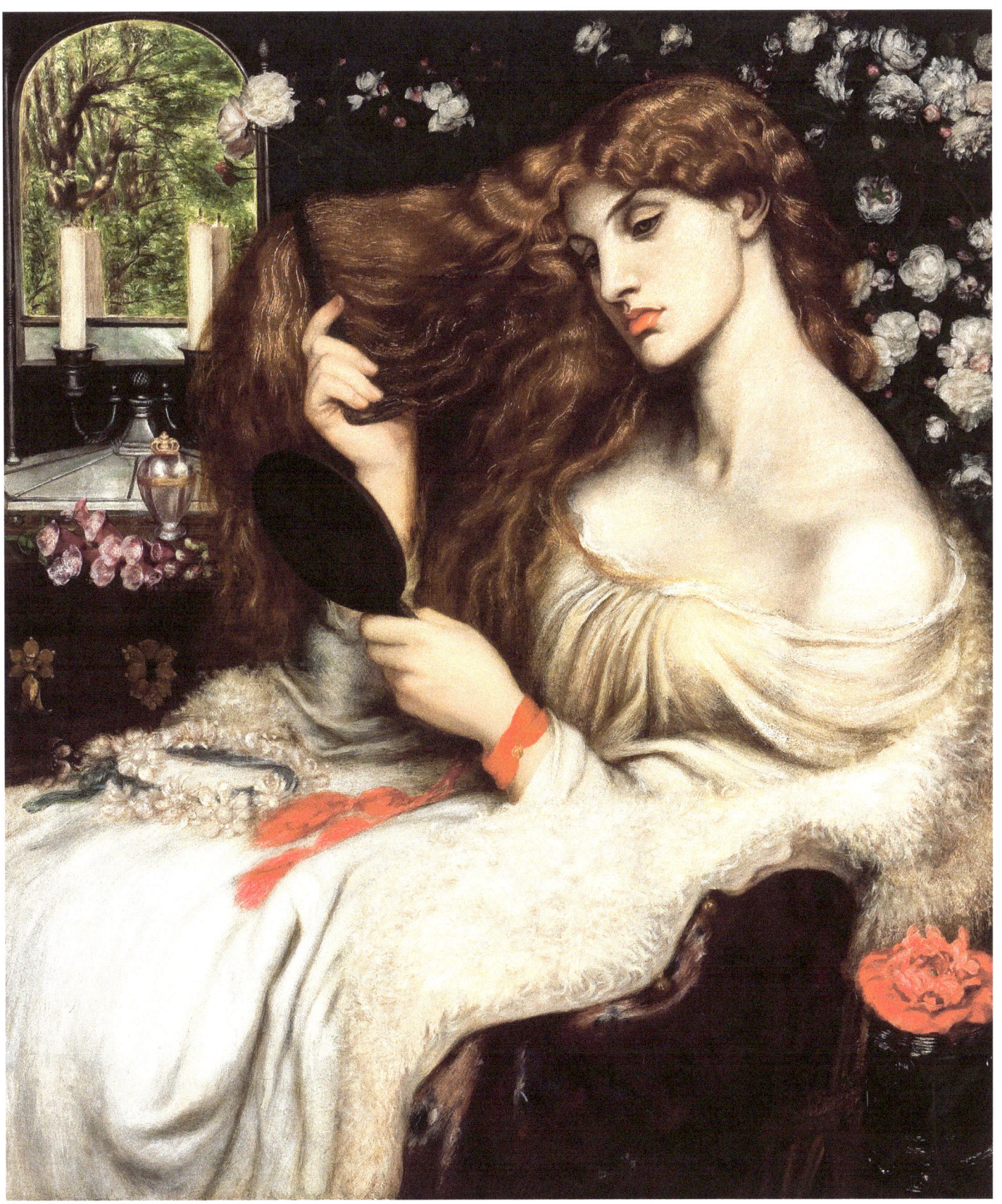

Fig. 15. Dante Gabriel Rossetti, *Lady Lilith*, 1866–68 (altered 1872–73), oil on canvas, 991 x 864 mm, Delaware Art Museum, Samuel and Mary Bancroft Memorial, 1935-29

The mythological Lilith was Adam's sensual first wife, "the witch he loved before the gift of Eve" according to Rossetti's sonnet "Lilith (For a Picture)," published in *Poems* in 1870 and later renamed "Body's Beauty" in *The House of Life* (1881), where it was paired with the sonnet "Soul's Beauty" that had been "Sibylla Palmifera (For a Picture)" in *Poems*.

In her collection of his work, *Fragments of Prose and Poetry* (1904) Eveleen published her husband's undated sonnet "A White Witch," for the first time.[199] I argue that it, and the article by Myers on Rossetti into which it fed, have a bearing on the propinquity in Bancroft's home of *Lady Lilith* to Eveleen's portrait. In "A White Witch" Myers was imitating Rossetti in writing a sonnet to accompany a picture. The picture in question appears to be Millais's portrait of Eveleen, for he describes the effect of seeing it at the 1875 Academy.

> Eyes that the morning star outshine,
> Veiled with their arching shade!
> Eyes from whose amorous deeps divine
> Looks forth a stainless maid!
> Eyes that the painter's art in vain
> Erewhile had burnt upon my brain,-
> No longer look on mine, or nevermore refrain!
>
> Turn, turn that lustrous gaze away,
> Enchantress innocent!
> No angers in those lightnings play,
> No willing bolts are sent;-
> All childly free those glances fly,-
> Nor yet the less must droop and die
> The heart lost unaware, and won unconsciously.

Although Myers had admired Rossetti's sonnets since the late 1860s, one can conjecture that this, his own sonnet for a picture, was written in 1882, two years after his marriage.[200] The evidence of his diary shows that this was the year in which he was most absorbed by Rossetti, whose death in April of that year reignited his interest.

On May 14 he noted "Rossettis at Leylands."[201] *Lady Lilith* had been purchased by shipowner and art collector Frederick Leyland of 49 Princes Gate, Kensington, in 1869 and was not sold to Bancroft until 1892. It would therefore have been one of the pictures Myers saw at Leyland's home on May 14. In his diary, Myers notes that from May 20 until July 1882 he was working on an article entitled "Rossetti and the Religion of Beauty," which would be published in the *Cornhill* in February 1883.[202] The July 10 entry states that Rossetti's peacock screen had been delivered to his home in Cambridge. Myers must have bought the screen, which figures in the background of another of Leyland's Rossettis, *Monna Rosa* (1867, private collection), in the sale of the contents of Rossetti's Cheyne Walk home on July 5–7,1882. On January 3 and 20 of the following year, he records visits to the Rossetti exhibitions at the Royal Academy and the Burlington Fine Arts Club, but there is no doubt that "Rossetti and the Religion of Beauty" was written in response to Leyland's pictures rather than to the two posthumous shows. He may in fact have withheld it from publication to coincide with them and simply updated it with his single reference to the Academy presentation.[203]

In his article Myers argued that as the study of art moved toward "the desire to extract the utmost secret, the occult message, from all the phenomena of Life and Being," so Rossetti's pictures, instead of being deemed merely sensual, should be understood as Platonic symbols of this ideal Love, love as worship.[204] They were evidence that an ideal form of love could exist, based not on the love of a single woman, "[t]here need be no exclusiveness in the loves of the spirit," but on the generalized love of beauty itself, "the highest things are also the loveliest."[205] Apart from the fact that with this theory he neatly exculpated himself for simultaneously loving Eveleen and Annie Marshall, Myers's article played a large part in transforming Rossetti's reputation, gravely damaged by Robert Buchanan's 1871 critique of his women as immoral or "fleshly," into that of one whose aim was a purely aesthetic, nonethical ideal.²⁰⁶

"A White Witch," which symbolically unites in Eveleen the soul and the body's beauty, spiritual, and sexual power, is Myers's own version of the aesthetic his article had constructed around Rossetti. Even the word "witch" of the title recalls Rossetti's use of it to describe the sensual Lilith in "Body's Beauty."²⁰⁷ Drawing on Rossetti's pairing of "Body's Beauty" with "Soul's Beauty" in *The House of Life*, Myers mines the same contrast of colors as Rossetti to illustrate the intermingling of the sexual and the spiritual. Eveleen, his white witch, wears red in the portraits of her, while in the paintings for which Rossetti's sonnets were written Lilith (Body's Beauty) wears virginal white, and her antithesis, Soul's Beauty, in *Sibylla Palmifera* (1865–70, National Museums Liverpool), passionate red.²⁰⁸ With his sonnet Myers is following the Rossetti paradigm to the letter.

In a passage in "Rossetti and the Religion of Beauty," Myers, describing Rossetti's women as ranging from "demon" to "angel," places Lilith, "whose beauty is destruction," paramount in the category of demon. Under "angel", on the other hand, he cites "the "maiden pre-elect," type of the love whose look regenerates and whose assumption lifts to heaven."²⁰⁹ In the first stanza of "A White Witch" Eveleen is a "stainless maid," while the word "regenerates" also links to Eveleen, for in the same year of 1882 Myers dedicated his book of poems *The Renewal of Youth*, "To

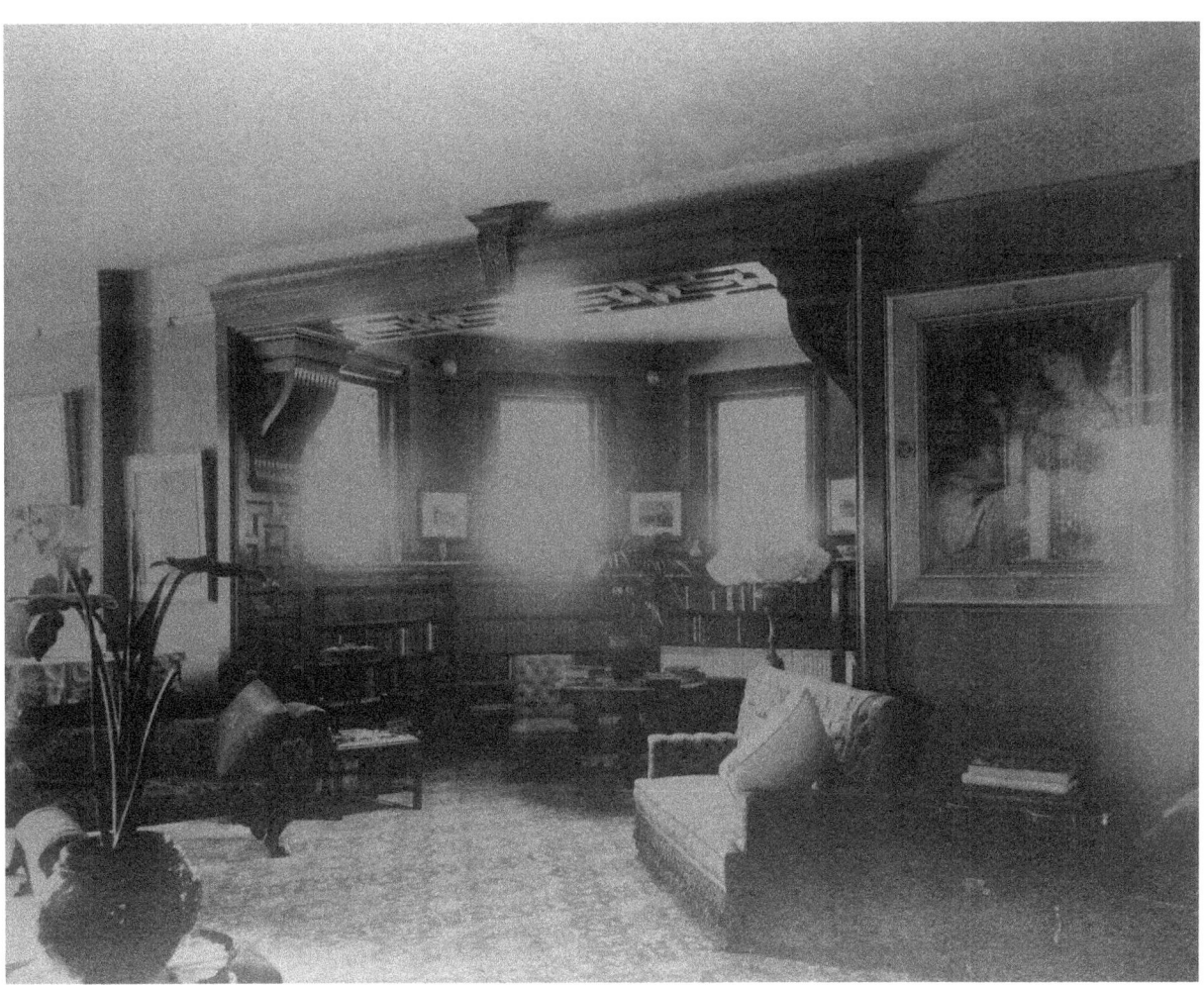

Fig. 16. *Drawing Room Alcove in Rockford, Home of Samuel Bancroft Jr.,* c. 1893, photographic print, Delaware Art Museum, Samuel and Mary R. Bancroft Pre-Raphaelite Manuscript Collection. *Lady Lilith* by Dante Gabriel Rossetti is on the right.

my wife." Eveleen, therefore, is not only an innocent maid, but also something more active, an agent of renewal and regeneration, his "Eve [...] leading me into Eden". Taking the passage as a whole, Myers's conclusion is not that Eveleen's nature confines her to this angelic type or opposes her to Lilith, but that there is no moral distinction between Lilith, "the witch he loved before the gift of Eve," and the maid, both being facets of ideal Love. In the second stanza of "A White Witch," indeed, the stainless maid has moved to become an enchantress, albeit an innocent one. With "A White Witch," Myers linked Eveleen to *Lady Lilith* many years before Bancroft did so.

Myers died in 1901 and probably never knew that Bancroft had hung the sweetly innocent portrait of Eveleen in the same room as the voluptuous and experienced *Lady Lilith* (fig. 16). It was, however, the pervasive influence of his article on Rossetti that made Bancroft the type of collector who, in seeing both as aspects of the ideal, could hang the two works together. The pictures even have a slight visual resemblance, with both subjects leaning back against an abundance of flowers. Watts had seen *Lady Lilith* in Rossetti's studio in the 1860s and his "words were few, but he gazed intently at the new picture," Mrs. Barrington tells us.[210] The Delaware portrait is arguably the most Rossetti-like of Watts's paintings of women and in the light of Myers's writings can be understood as an apt pairing with *Lady Lilith*.

In his article on Rossetti, Myers alluded to what he called "the look" or "some union of strange and puissant physical loveliness with depth and remoteness of gaze." He also added, "The most direct appeals, the most penetrating reminiscences, come to the worshipper of Beauty from a woman's eyes."[211] It is clear that Rossetti's mesmerising women, were, as much as his own belief in psychic force, behind Myers's obsession with Eveleen's portraits. Yet in "A White Witch," a poem also preoccupied with "the look," he asks Eveleen to turn her "lustrous gaze away." How did Eveleen reconcile these conflicting messages?

EVELEEN, THE INDEPENDENT PHOTOGRAPHER

The older, married Eveleen was a very different character from the demure child her London family largely continued to think her, although both Millais and Watts had sensed, and suggested in their portraits, the passionate, determined woman of later years. By 1900, when Bancroft made his purchase, she had become a relatively well-known portrait photographer, having originally taken up the activity in 1888 to photograph her children. The years 1889 to 1892 seem to have been the height of her renown. Her photograph of Dolly, "bride of the month," appeared in the first of the series "Photographs of the Month" in W. T. Stead's *Review of Reviews* in 1890.[212] This and another picture of Dolly taken from behind were not for sale but other subject photos are listed at prices of 10s 6d and £1 11s 6d. The list was drawn up by Fred, not Eveleen, "too quick," Evy thought.[213]

Her studies of their children—Leo, Silvia and Harold—filled her husband's library at Leckhampton, where she had perhaps placed them to remind Myers of the reality of family life when he was in danger, as all too often, of being overtaken by SPR work.[214] By becoming a photographer she turned the tables on her portraitists, refusing any longer to be the object of their scrutiny or to engage the male gaze. One perceives the conventional feelings of modesty that had overtaken her after her engagement, the desire to be appraised only by her husband's eyes, evolving into the more modern assertiveness of one who refuses to allow her beauty to be used in any sort of transaction, whether sexual or spiritual. As her husband had, for his own reasons, enjoined her to do, she is, quite independently, turning her "lustrous gaze away." Eveleen's sitters were also, as often as not, encouraged to cast their eyes down or to the side just as Dolly had posed her for the Delaware portrait. The result is that the psychological power of many of her photographs comes from the fact that her sitter is, as Rossetti had described Lady Lilith in "Body's Beauty," "subtly of herself contemplative." In his painting Rossetti had used the device of Lilith gazing at her own image in a mirror to suggest the phrase, the implication being that she was holding fast to her inner self even as the artist created a material version of her for external consumption. In fact, of course, the gazing in a mirror, far from being a self-generated female activity, was also part of the male artist's creation. Eveleen escapes this circularity when, as a woman photographer, she photographs her female subjects with Lilith's downcast glance.

In 1890 her personal Rossetti connection amounted to little more than having one of her photographs of Robert Browning engraved to accompany an article in the *Magazine of Art* by W. M. Rossetti, the artist's brother. Rossetti was not, as it happened, particularly enthusiastic about Eveleen's work.[215] In fact it was Marion Spielmann, the magazine's editor and a great admirer of Eveleen's portrait by Millais, who was eager to promote her.[216] The following January Spielmann solicited two of her pictures, with others by Julia Margaret Cameron, to illustrate an article called "The Artistic Aspects of Figure Photography" by the naturalistic photographer P. H. Emerson.[217] The *Magazine of Art* was, according to Emerson, noted for its support of artistic photography, but in his contrarious text he declared Cameron's photographs largely failures and failed to comment on Eveleen's at all.[218] It is clear that Emerson was publishing in the wrong place, for shortly afterwards, in a black-bordered pamphlet entitled "The Death of Naturalistic Photography," he repudiated photography as a fine art altogether.[219] Unabashed, Eveleen wrote to her husband in July that she found Emerson "tiresome."[220]

She had more affinity with the Linked Ring, founded in 1892 by, among others, Cameron's son Henry, to promote the pictorial aspects of photography over the technical, and is said, unlike Emerson, to have exhibited with them in the early 1890s.[221] She also found a more sympathetic critic than either Rossetti or Emerson in Myers's friend, the poet and critic John Addington Symonds.[222] Writing of Eveleen's work in the April 1891 issue of *Sun Artists*, a quarterly devoted to artistic photography, Symonds stated that work like hers had "greater documentary value, deeper psychological veracity, than the best of paintings" because it did not need to take pains to catch a likeness but instead could concentrate on what the photographer "thinks and feels about the man."[223] This bold claim appeared to place Eveleen the photographer at a more advanced stage as a portraitist than a painter like Millais. Eveleen took a less exalted view of her abilities. In 1896, after speaking very confidently to Marie Belloc of her skills and her powers of perception, she concluded the interview with the conventional opinion that photography was subordinate to fine art, little more than a factual aid to the artist, even though "it need not stand in the way of the higher imaginative truth which only the artist's own mind can put into his work."[224]

Eveleen's modest assessment notwithstanding, recent scholars have agreed that the best of her photographs are as sensitive and searching as a portrait by Millais or Watts.[225] Indeed, they seem to draw on her girlhood experience of sitting for those artists. Her account of capturing Adelaide Passingham in 1889 shows how the atmosphere she created was informal, *carnavalesque*, Bacchanalian even. There may still be a male observer, but he is merely her infant son, Harold, while she, the photographer, concentrates on her sitter, blurring the lines between them as they parade their clothing and girlishly loosen their hair:

> Had a splendid morning of Adelaid. —8— grand heads. 12 10—plates the largest all good, some superb she staid till 3.30 then drove with me in the town. [...] Harold greatly admired Adelaid and said to her 'quelle belle dame! [...] and after a little Comme elle a de beaux cheveux!!—si beaux. We looked so

strange a bunch A. with all her hair down & in the pink silk. —I in canary yellow gauze with my black hair down!—[226]

The loose clothes recall the classical Wattsian ideal, outside modern fashion (fig. 17). The loose hair, on the other hand, suggests not just the innocence of girlhood, but the sensuality of Lilith. Perhaps it is also Eveleen, pace Myers, allowing the animal, Darwinian note to enter in, as if in homage to Huxley. The downcast gaze, meanwhile, which I have argued reflects Eveleen's mature preoccupation with women engrossed in their own thoughts, also resembles and perhaps even owes its origins to that adopted by her father, Charles Tennant, in the photograph Eveleen pasted into her childhood album (p. 15). For Eveleen, as for Dolly, the dead man's spirit was a real and constant presence.

There are ways, however, in which her work is also similar to that of Myers, ways in which they appear to be working in partnership. The two photographs she took in 1889 of the French medium Léonie Boulenger, for example, one in a trance with eyes closed and the other alert with eyes wide open, must represent her efforts to track alongside Myers the scientific reality of invisible phenomena.[227] They seem to converge with his growing interest in using experimental psychology to assess trance states. William James, the Harvard professor of philosophy who taught his first experimental psychology course at Harvard in 1875–76 and published *Principles of Psychology* in 1890, described Myers as "a psychologist who worked upon lines hardly admitted by the more academic branch of the profession to be legitimate," but a psychologist all the same.[228] Eveleen's experience of having her character analysed by Millais and Watts as well as her fascination with the process as she developed her own work as a portrait photographer made her, as Symonds had pointed out in 1891, something of a psychologist too. Her pictures are, like Myers's research, part of the emerging discipline of psychology.

Eveleen herself remarked that through having had various mediums stay at Leckhampton she had come "to realise the psychological complexities of mediumship."[229] Her 1890 portrait of American medium Leonora Piper demonstrates more precisely where she positioned herself on this (fig. 18). James, who was closely involved with Myers in his spiritual research, had in 1885, after the death of his son, become interested in Piper, attended sittings with her, and promoted her name. In 1889 he recommended that she be sent to England so that the SPR could investigate her mediumship thoroughly. Alta Piper, Leonora's daughter, tells us that Eveleen welcomed her to Leckhampton, with the slight lisp which must have been part of her charm, "Why, Mrs. Piper, you are not at all like what I expected! I thought you would wear your hair in frizettes and be dressed in magenta!"[230] She evidently had an artist's eye for dress as a marker of social class. Indeed, as Henry James was brave enough to remark about her to Myers, "How she must miss Richmond Terrace!"[231] This was in November 1890, a few weeks after James had reluctantly agreed to read his brother William's paper on Mrs. Piper's spiritualistic trances to the SPR.[232] In qualification of James's view of Eveleen as a worldly creature, however, the photograph of Piper is purged of all realistic detail, of all that might have appealed to a Millais or a James. It is distinctly more Wattsian, with the pose and the loosened hair both reminiscent of his Delaware portrait, but with the last remaining material notes removed. Eveleen's photograph concentrates our attention, makes us think and work, but then leaves our judgment suspended. Are we to understand that Piper is in a trance or are we expected to sound the depths of her character? The sitter herself remains enigmatic, looks away, and withholds.

When the photograph was taken, Piper was staying at Leckhampton and just then shaking the serenity of

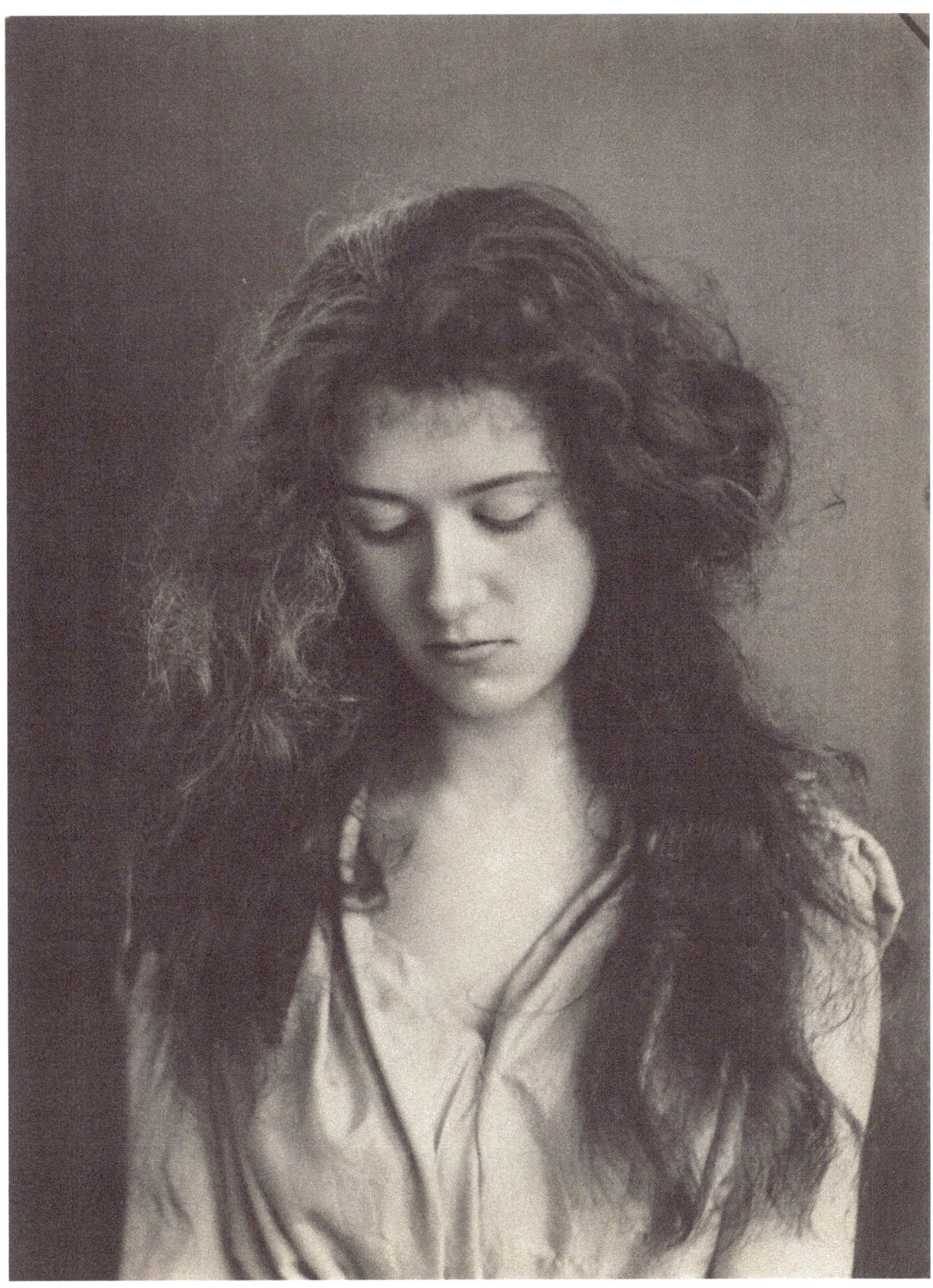

Fig. 17. Eveleen Myers (née Tennant), *Adelaide Passingham (1867–1954)*, 1889, platinum print, 293 x 222 mm, National Portrait Gallery, London, NPG Ax36315

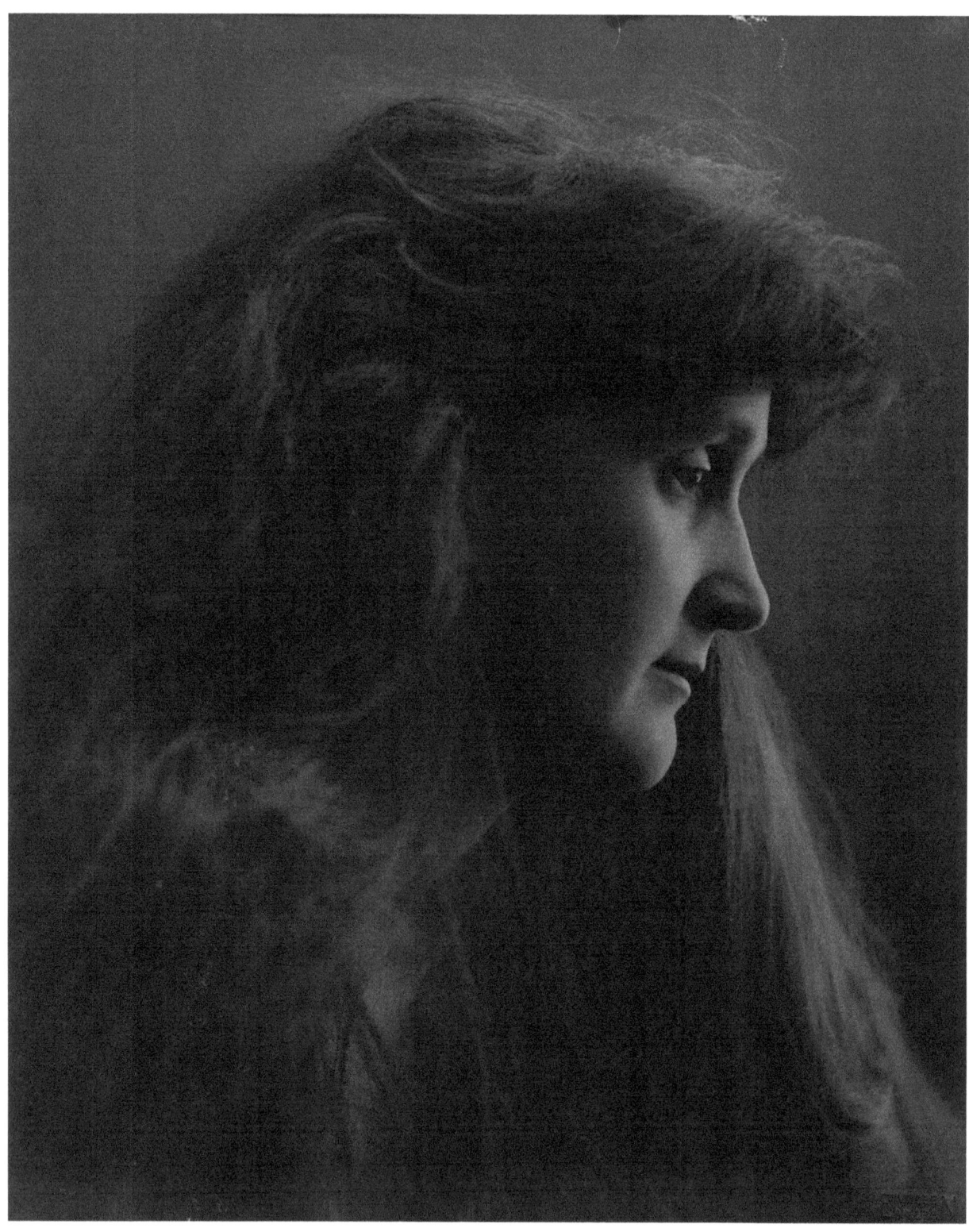

Fig. 18. Eveleen Myers (née Tennant), *Leonora Piper*, 1890, platinum print, 275 x 225 mm, National Portrait Gallery, London, NPG x87656

the household by claiming to have made contact with Annie Marshall. Eveleen, whom Myers noted in his diary was affected by these séances, had every reason to wish to take the measure of her houseguest.[233] In 1901–2, after her husband's death, she went to the United States to have sittings with her and judge for herself whether the messages the medium was claiming to receive from Myers were genuine, but could not even then be completely sure.[234]

On the whole, despite the occasional sense of shared professional interest, where Myers sought, Eveleen did not find. She certainly never claimed to have photographed a spirit, as Myers may have hoped she would, if his 1886 advice to a Miss Morton, who contacted the SPR with a case of possible spirit visitation, is anything to go by. Myers told Morton that she should try to photograph the apparition to test its material reality.[235] Such was the practice of his SPR colleague, scientific chemist William Crookes, who, having begun his career as a photographer in the 1840s, claimed in 1874 to have captured the so-called spirit Katie King.[236]

In 1888, when Eveleen decided to take up photography, it was not, significantly, to Crookes that she went for tuition but to the photographer and lens-maker Albert Dew-Smith, who was partner to Charles Darwin's son Horace in the Cambridge Scientific Instrument Company.[237] Dew-Smith and Darwin founded a new firm in 1881 and Dew-Smith enlarged it to encompass photography and lithographic printing. He was a Trinity man like Myers but differed significantly in being linked to the scientific materialism of Thomas Henry Huxley, with whom he had founded the Physiological Society in 1876. Dew-Smith must further have endeared himself to Eveleen by his interest in the arts, for his personal collection included works not only by Rossetti, but by Burne-Jones, whom the Tennants knew well. J. J. Thomson, a fellow of Trinity in 1880, described Dew-Smith as "of a type not often found in our Society, familiar with life in London and especially with Club life."[238] This was just the sort of contact Eveleen had been looking for in Cambridge. She wrote under the portrait photograph she took of Dew-Smith (fig. 19), to which, behind his head, she had added a rather solid halo, "I have him as a saint—my great friend."[239]

Over the years Myers made slightly disparaging remarks about photography, which may have

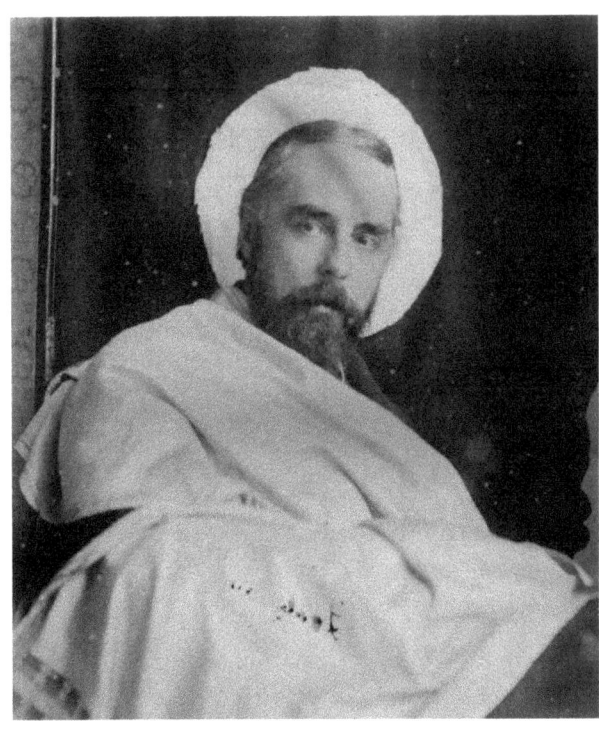

Fig. 19. Eveleen Myers (née Tennant), *Albert George Dew-Smith*, 1888, albumen print, 170 x 145 mm, National Portrait Gallery, London, NPG Ax68568

been directed at Eveleen's interest in it and at her concentration on the material world, remarks too which may have provoked her own depreciation of its importance to Marie Belloc. The sketch Jean-Jacques Henner made of her in January 1880, for example, Myers described to Eveleen as "far better than any photograph," while in an article of 1889 he declared Millais's portrait of Tennyson the best rendering of the poet, superior to the mere fidelity of photographs, before superimposing on to this rather faint compliment his own grandiose description of Tennyson as a powerful visionary, the "prophet [...] of a Spiritual Universe."[240] In his 1887 story *The Canterville Ghost*, which Myers must have known because it names him and explicitly satirises his psychical research, Oscar Wilde, who was an old friend of Dolly and Eveleen's, identified portrait photography with a modern, healthy, American materialistic outlook. Hiram B. Otis, the no-nonsense American minister, having bought Canterville Chase, an English country house haunted for centuries, replaced the Canterville family pictures with "large Saroni photographs" of himself and his wife.[241] Napoleon Sarony was an American photographer who had photographed Wilde in New York in 1882.[242] It is interesting that it was the very year after Wilde's story appeared that Eveleen nailed her banners to the materialist flag and took up portrait photography herself. That Myers feared it, and possibly by analogy feared Eveleen's lens, Eveleen's eyes, being turned on him after his death is forcibly suggested by his 1893 description of how repugnant to him was the thought that "all things thought and felt, as well as all things done, are somehow photographed imperishably upon the Universe, and that my whole past will probably lie open to those with whom I have to do."[243]

Eveleen's choice of photography as her independent occupation appears, according to these hints from Myers, to distance her from his non-material concerns and realign her to the Millais aesthetic of resemblance. This is not quite the full story, however, for as we have seen in our analysis of her Piper photograph, the intervening years since sitting for Millais had changed Eveleen, and given her work a maturity of understanding, an inward-looking depth, which must have derived partly from Myers himself. She wrote to her husband in January 1892, "I see through people—I see what they are & what they want & what they pretend to be."[244] She had also absorbed a great deal from Watts, and having sat both to him and to Millais, was in the unusual position of being able to unite in herself their different points of view. As Spielmann pointed out, "[N]ot many sitters have been so brilliantly immortalized by two such distinguished masters."[245] The experience of having her portrait painted, of being scrutinized by and becoming intimate with two searching minds, had taught Eveleen something about the complexity of human nature and the potential of human relations that her husband, for all his intellectual efforts, could not entirely fathom. Then, due to the strange circumstances of her marriage, she had also grown through suffering. There is a particularly apposite passage in *The Portrait of a Lady* (1881), the novel Henry James began just after hearing of Eveleen's engagement to Myers, when, shortly after her arrival in England, Ralph Touchett tours the picture gallery of his father's country house with Isabel Archer. She holds up a candle to the images, studies them closely and impresses her cousin by her "natural taste."[246] Immediately afterward, however, she relapses into girlish immaturity by demanding all the same if there isn't a ghost in the house:

> Ralph shook his head sadly. "I might show it to you, but you would never see it. The privilege isn't given to everyone; it's not enviable. It has never been seen by a young, happy, innocent person like you. You must have suffered first, have suffered greatly, have gained some miserable knowledge. In that way your eyes are opened to it. I saw it long ago," said Ralph, smiling.[247]

Even if James did not in the least mean what Myers did by the phrase, Isabel will learn in time, as did Eveleen, to see ghosts.

Although this acquired insight is precisely what would make Eveleen such a strong portraitist, the fact of her work does not seem to have been communicated to Bancroft. In 1906 Agnew's, in a statement full of inaccuracies, designed to appeal to the collector's thirst for gossip about the personalities of the English art world, described her solely in terms of her more famous relations as "the wife of Professor

Myers of Cambridge University" and "a sister of Lady Stanley who was used by Millais as his model when he painted 'Yes or No.'"[248] Bancroft was probably also left ignorant of an intimate connection that would have interested him as the picture started its life in the United States. His great-uncle, Jacob Bright, who owned the cotton mills near Manchester where Bancroft's father had learned the business, was the father of Radical politician John Bright.[249] Bright had been a great friend to Charles Tennant and his family, Evy included. Her portrait was not, therefore, passing entirely among strangers.

Eveleen, the sister her family had assumed was merely sweet and decorative, succeeded as an adult in rebutting that definition. Through her impressive catalogue of photographic portraits she achieved, for a while, greater independent renown than her dominating sister, Lady Stanley.[250] The laurel wreath of distinction, hinted at by Watts in his picture, ultimately was hers. Yet it is clear that both young women, having burst into society by means of a series of extraordinary and attention-grabbing portraits, found their mature contentment in deflecting the appraising look away from themselves. There is much to ponder in the Delaware portrait before dropping one's gaze and moving away.

ARCHIVAL SOURCES

Dorothy Tennant Journals, The Henry M. Stanley Archives, collection of the King Baudouin Foundation, held in trust at the Royal Museum for Central Africa, Tervuren, Belgium (DTJ)

Samuel and Mary R. Bancroft Pre-Raphaelite Manuscript Collection, Helen Farr Sloan Library & Archives, Delaware Art Museum (Bancroft Collection)

Archives, Corpus Christi College, Cambridge

Marlay Collection, Manuscripts and Special Collections, University of Nottingham (Marlay Collection)

Myers Papers with acknowledgment to The Master and Fellows of Trinity College, Cambridge (Trinity College Myers)

Thos. Agnew & Sons, Picture Stock Books 1898–1904, National Gallery, London (NGA)

Photographs by Eveleen Myers, 1880s–1910s, National Portrait Gallery Archives (NPG)

Watts, M. S. "Catalogue of the Works of G.F. Watts, compiled by his widow.'" 3 MS volumes c.1910. Archives, Watts Gallery, Compton (Watts 1910)

The original spelling and punctuation of Eveleen and Dorothy's manuscripts has been preserved.

Permission to quote from manuscript material has been kindly granted by the Helen Farr Sloan Library & Archives, Delaware Art Museum; the Masters and Fellows of Trinity College, Cambridge; the University of Nottingham, Manuscripts and Special Collections and the Henry M. Stanley Archives, collection of the King Baudouin Foundation, held in trust at the Royal Museum for Central Africa, Belgium.

ABBREVIATIONS

EM (Eveleen Myers), FM (Frederic Myers), DT (Dorothy Tennant), ET (Eveleen Tennant), GT (Gertrude Tennant), GFW (George Frederic Watts).

Dorothy Tennant Journals, The Henry M. Stanley Archives, collection of the King Baudouin Foundation, held in trust at the Royal Museum for Central Africa, Tervuren, Belgium (DTJ)

Samuel and Mary R. Bancroft Pre-Raphaelite Manuscript Collection, Helen Farr Sloan Library & Archives, Delaware Art Museum (Bancroft Collection)

Archives, Corpus Christi College, Cambridge

Marlay Collection, Manuscripts and Special Collections, University of Nottingham (Marlay Collection)

Myers Papers with acknowledgment to The Master and Fellows of Trinity College, Cambridge (Trinity College Myers)

Thos. Agnew & Sons, Picture Stock Books 1898–1904, National Gallery, London (NGA)

Photographs by Eveleen Myers, 1880s-1910s, National Portrait Gallery Archives (NPG)

Watts, M.S. "Catalogue of the Works of G.F. Watts, compiled by his widow.'" 3 MS volumes c.1910. Archives, Watts Gallery, Compton (Watts 1910)

NOTES

[1] Delaware Art Museum, Samuel and Mary R. Bancroft Memorial, 1935-4.

[2] Eveleen Tennant, November 21, 1856–March 2, 1937; Dorothy Tennant, March 22, 1855–October 5, 1926.

[3] Cadoxton Lodge, bought by George Tennant in 1823, was sold in 1963 and demolished in 1966. Keith Tucker, *Chronicle of Cadoxton* (Neath: Historical Projects, 1994).

[4] For the Tennant Canal, see Tucker 1994, 138–45. It remained profitable until the 1890s. Commercial traffic ceased about 1934.

[5] DTJ 5931, October 24, 1881. David Waller, *The Magnificent Mrs. Tennant: The Adventurous Life of Gertrude Tennant, Victorian Grande Dame* (New Haven: Yale University Press, 2009), 180.

[6] Waller 2009, 184; DTJ 5926, May 31, 1876.

[7] Dorothy Tennant Journals, Henry M. Stanley Archives, collection of the King Baudouin Foundation, held in trust at the Royal Museum for Central Africa, Tervuren, Belgium.

[8] DTJ 5926. April 12, 1876. A photograph in Eveleen's album at the NPG of Alice as a girl, with her long hair loose, is annotated in Eveleen's hand: "Elsie Tennant sister of Dorothy & us all See her Lovely Hair!" EM, Album 200, NPG Ax 68339. Eveleen's photographic albums and a number of her photographs were acquired by the NPG from Peter Myers in 1991 and constitute the major public holding of her work.

[9] DTJ 5926, February 4 [1877]; February 24, 1877.

[10] DTJ 5926, May 31, 1876.

[11] For Gertrude's upbringing in France, see Waller 2009.

[12] Waller 2009, 179.

[13] "I'm afraid I shant go to Perugini's any more as he asks 30 Guineas a Quarter." DTJ 5922, December 11, 1871. Originally from Naples, Perugini would marry Charles Dickens's daughter Kate, also a painter, in 1874.

[14] The Slade opened at University College, London, in 1871. Its first professor, Edward Poynter, studied in Paris under Charles Gleyre and was anxious to introduce the advantages of the French system in England. Equal opportunities to study from the partially draped model were accordingly offered to men and women in both separate and mixed classes. There was no competitive test of entry.

[15] Alta L. Piper, *The Life and Work of Mrs. Piper* (London: Kegan Paul, Trench, Trubner & Co, 1919), 53.

[16] DTJ 5925, February 11, 1876.

[17] DTJ 5925, February 11, 1876.

[18] DTJ 5926, April 30, 1876; May 4, 1876. On May 2 Eveleen had sung "some quaint old songs" to Turgenev and Flaubert out of Weckerlin's *Echos du temps passé* (1855). Pauline Viardot (1821–1910) taught at the Paris Conservatoire from 1870 to 1883. She saw Eveleen on May 4 and offered her free lessons.

[19] Emile Durand-Gréville, *Entretiens de J-J Henner, Notes Prises par Emile Durand-Gréville, après ses conversations avec J-J Henner* (1878–1888) (Paris: Librairie Alphonse Lemerre, 1925), January 13, 1880, 89. During the winters of 1879 and 1880 Dolly attended the atelier des dames at 17 quai Voltaire in Paris under Charles Carolus-Duran (1837–1917) and Jean-Jacques Henner (1829–1905). In the second winter she was also a private pupil of Henner at his atelier in the Place Pigalle. See Isabelle de Lannoy, "Jean-Jacques Henner et 'l'atelier des dames' […]" in Françoise Sarret et al., *Marie Petiet: être femme peintre au 19e siècle*, Musée Petiet, Limoux (Milan: Silvano Editoriale, 2014), 13–17, exhibition catalogue. Durand-Gréville's comment reads: "One of the daughters, with fine, energetic features and slightly unruly black hair, sings, with real feeling, if not with method; she is a pupil of Mme Viardot."

[20] "Mrs. F. W. H. Myers as remembered by her granddaughter Deenagh Goold-Adams," typescript with Myers Papers, Trinity College Cambridge, Add. Ms.a/401, copy in NPG, 1.

[21] DTJ 5926, June 26, 1876.

[22] Alan Gauld, "Myers, Frederic William Henry (1843–1901)." *Oxford Dictionary of National Biography* (Oxford University Press, 2004). Evidence that Eveleen pursued her interest in music to some extent after her marriage is provided in a letter she wrote to her husband on August 5, 1887. "This morning I went to Mrs. Jebbs & did some music with Miss Dupuy she has a very pretty voice." Trinity College Myers 6/118. Mrs. Jebb, who lived at Springfield, Queens Road, Cambridge, was the American wife of Cambridge classicist Richard Claverhouse Jebb and aunt to Maud Dupuy, whose family were from Pennsylvania. Maud married Charles Darwin's son George in 1884 and came to live at Newnham Grange. Her sister Ella is probably the Miss Dupuy in question here. For a photograph of her see Margaret Keynes, *A House by the River. Newnham Grange to Darwin College* (Cambridge: privately printed, 1984), facing 64.

[23] FM to Henry Sidgwick, January 1, 1879 [1880], Trinity College Myers, 12/51.

[24] "My hair was down." Annotation by EM on invitation card from Hamilton Aïdé to FM, Trinity College Myers, 25/118.

[25] Trinity College Myers, 25/118. DTJ 5929, December 7, 1879. 'The Miss Tennants at Hamilton Aïdés." [November] 14,[1879], Diary of F. W. H. Myers. Trinity College Myers, 14/1.

[26] Diary of F. W. H. Myers, Trinity College Myers, 14/1.

[27] FM to Miss Tennant [Dolly], December 4, 1879. Trinity College Myers 25/130(1). "Virgil." *Fortnightly Review 31* (February 1879), 163–96.

[28] DTJ 5929.

[29] FM to Miss Tennant [Dolly], December 15, 1879. Trinity College Myers, 25/131.

[30] Myers's diary entry for December 23, 1879, reads "Mrs Mohl's: E's lunch: she bursts into room: repeats poetry: camomile tea, made Acrostics on Boulevards." That for the next day reads "E. at Caro's lecture. Sainte Chapelle. Palais de Justice: Louvre. Théâtre Français. Coquelin in box." "Caro" is probably Carolus-Duran, see note 19, while the actor Benoît-Constant Coquelin was a friend of the Tennants. On Christmas Day Myers got a further taste of the Tennants' Bohemianism when he called at their hotel and found, as he noted, Eveleen in her dressing gown. Trinity College Myers 14/1.

[31] Henry James to GT, February 16, 1880, Trinity College Myers 25/144, repr. in *The Complete Letters of Henry James, 1878–1880*, vol. 2, ed. Pierre A. Walker and Greg. W. Zacharias (Lincoln and London: University of Nebraska Press, 2015), 127.

[32] Waller 2009, 212.

[33] "Stanley's Wedding," *Poverty Bay Herald* (New Zealand), July 21, 1890.

[34] 1829 is the date of birth given by his literary executor R. Warwick Bond in *The Marlay Letters 1778–1820* (London: Constable & Co., 1937), 1831 that given in N.W. Goodison and Denys Sutton, "French, German Spanish," *Catalogue of Paintings*, vol. 1. (Cambridge: Syndics of the Fitzwilliam Museum, Cambridge, 1960), 175, *The Times* death announcement and *Who Was Who*. As Marlay's sister Catherine was born in 1831, after her father's death, however, 1829 is the more likely birthdate for Marlay.

[35] Thomas O'Reilly, P. P. Kinnegad, to the editor of the *Westmeath Gazette*, March 8, 1880, http://www.askaboutireland.ie/reading-room/history-heritage/big-houses-of-ireland/belvedere-house-co.-westm/charles-brinsley-marlay/.

[36] Designed in 1827 by Edward Poynter's architect father, Ambrose.

[37] Lucilla Burn, *The Fitzwilliam Museum: A History* (London: Philip Wilson Publishers, 2016), 134–39.

[38] Mary Lutyens, ed., *Effie in Venice: Unpublished letters of Mrs. John Ruskin Written from Venice between 1849 and 1852* (London: Pallas Editions, 1999), 199–200, http://blogs.nottingham.ac.uk/manuscripts/2014/10/16/effie-lady-eastlake-and-the-evidence-in-the-archives/.

[39] The correspondence between Catherine Louisa Marlay and her son Brinsley is in the Marlay Collection, University of Nottingham, Manuscripts and Special Collections.

[40] Henry James, *The Bostonians* (London: Penguin Books, 2000), 132. The text is that of the 1886 three-volume edition.

[41] DTJ 5926, April 10, 1876.

[42] DTJ 5926, July 5, 1876. Madame Elise (Elizabeth Marie Louise Jaeger, 1829–1913) ran her business from 170 Regent Street, London.

[43] DTJ 5926, July 8, 1876.

[44] DTJ 5926, December 23, 1876.

[45] DTJ 5926, December 16, 1876.

[46] DTJ 5929, July 21, 1879. Dolly gives the rejected suitors' names: Mr. Wyndham Stanhope, Colonel Frazer, and Mr. Fairfield.

[47] GT to C. B. Marlay, August 5, 1879. My3538 (1), Marlay Collection.

[48] The Tennants were presented to the former Emperor Napoleon III and his wife, Eugénie, at Chislehurst in 1871, shortly after the couple's exile to England. Waller 2009, 175–77. Charles Frederick Worth's premises were at 7 rue de la Paix, Paris.

[49] Dolly gives a long and vivid description of the visit in DTJ 5926, May 4, 1876, and adds a sketch of her dress and cap. Watts's first skullcap was made for him by Annie Prinsep in 1874. Veronica Franklin Gould, *G. F. Watts. The Last Great Victorian* (New Haven: Yale University Press for the Paul Mellon Centre for Studies in British Art, 2004), 390, 124n.

[50] DTJ 5926, July 1, 1876.

[51] GFW to ET, January 3, 1875. Trinity College Myers, 25/2.

[52] DTJ 5925, March 13, 1875.

[53] DTJ 5926, August 28, 1876.

[54] GFW, The Briary, Freshwater, Isle of Wight to Charles H. Rickards, Old Trafford, Manchester, September 17, 1876. NPG; GFW/1/3/37.

[55] Mary Fraser Tytler became Mary Seton Watts on her marriage to the artist in 1886.

[56] "Catalogue of the Works of G. F. Watts, compiled by His Widow," MS vols., c. 1910, 156. (Archives, Watts Gallery, Compton). [Hereafter Watts 1910]. F. W. H. Myers manuscript draft autobiography dated June 4, 1893. Trinity College Myers, 26/63: 68.

[57] DTJ 5926, September 4, 1876. Anne Thackeray, *The Village on the Cliff* (1867), written 1865–66. She and her husband Richmond Ritchie were guests at Dolly's wedding to Stanley in 1890. Eveleen would make a photographic portrait of Anny's brother-in-law Leslie Stephen in about 1890 [NPG Ax36302] and in 1914 was one of the friends who subscribed to her portrait by Sargent. Hester Ritchie, ed., *Letters of Anne Thackeray Ritchie* (London: John Murray, 1924), 286.

[58] DTJ 5926, September 7, 1876. Fernside, Freshwater. Grace Aguilar (1816–1847), author of seven novels including *Home Influence: A Tale for Mothers and Daughters* (1850).

[59] DTJ 5926, September 7, 1876.

[60] M. S. Watts, *George Frederic Watts: The Annals of an Artist's Life* (London: Macmillan and Co., Ltd, 1912), vol. I, 298–99. Watts had bought the land on which the Briary was built in 1871. The house was designed by Philip Webb in 1872 and completed in 1873. Watts started using it, sharing it with his friends the Prinseps, from 1874, while retaining his London base at Little Holland House.

[61] DTJ 5926, September 10, 1876.

[62] Waller 2009, 191.

[63] DTJ 5926, October 27, 1876. Blanche Clogstoun (1862–1895), a relative of the Prinseps, was adopted by Watts in 1872.

[64] DTJ 5926, September 10, 1876.

[65] Gertrude's reaction to the Tate portrait is quoted in Waller 2009, 191.

[66] DTJ 5926, September 14, [1876]. On May 9, 1877, she wrote, "The truth is Signor is very fond of Eveleen and me, he quite clings to us, and he is at his merriest and his best when we are all in his studio." DTJ 5927. Annie Prinsep (1848–1933), the daughter of Charles Prinsep, Advocate General of Bengal, and his wife Louisa, had been living on the Isle of Wight with her aunt, Julia Margaret Cameron. In 1876 she would have been twenty-eight. See 49n.

[67] DTJ 5926, September 16, 1876.

[68] DTJ 5926.

[69] DTJ 5926.

[70] DTJ 5929, October 27, 1879.

[71] GFW to DT, Little Holland House, October 23, 1879. DTJ 5929, October 30, [18]79.

[72] DTJ 5929, November 11, 1879.

[73] DTJ 5929, November 19, 1879. GFW, "The Present Conditions of Art" (Nineteenth Century, 1880), repr. M. S. Watts 1912, vol. III, 148–90.

74 DTJ 5926, October 19, 1876.

75 DTJ 5929, November 19, 1879.

76 DTJ 5929, November 22, 1879.

77 DTJ 5929, November 22, 1879.

78 M.S. Watts, "Catalogue."

79 Having witnessed some of Charcot's experiments in hypnosis at the Salpêtrière in Paris in the mid-1880s Myers would become convinced that female hysteria or trance states could be reassessed using the tools of experimental psychology. FM, "Human Personality in the Light of Hypnotic Suggestion," *Proceedings of the Society for Psychical Research* 4 (1885), 1–24; Trevor Hamilton. Immortal Longings, F. W. H. Myers and the Victorian Search for Life after Death (Exeter: Imprint Academic, 2009), 152–57.

80 Quoted in Alan Gauld, *The Founders of Psychical Research* (London: Routledge & Kegan Paul, 1968), 136.

81 DTJ 5926, September 17, 1876.

82 J. Paul Getty Museum collection database.

83 Terence Pepper, *Edwardian Women Photographers. Eveleen Myers, Alice Hughes, Christina Broom and Olive Edis* (London: National Portrait Gallery, 1994).

84 Gertrude and Charles Tennant had fallen in love at Ryde on the Isle of Wight and were married there in 1847. Waller 2009, 98–108. Cameron was given her first camera in December 1863.

85 Marie A. Belloc, "An Interview with Mrs. F. W. H. Myers," *The Woman at Home, Annie S. Swan's Magazine* (June 1896), 763. The whereabouts of this photograph are unknown.

86 F. Bockrath, *Technical Examination Report: G. F. Watts, Portrait of Eveleen Tennant* (West Chester, PA: Barbara A. Buckley and Associates, April 30, 2021).

87 Debra N. Mancoff, *Flora Symbolica: Flowers in Pre-Raphaelite Art* (New York: Prestel, 2003), 26.

88 Marlay was from 1857 advised by Ninian Niven, curator of the Dublin Botanical Gardens, in a "quite stunning" redesign of the grounds of Belvedere House, his Irish home. Olive Sharkey, "Belvedere Restored," *Irish Arts Review* 19, no. 2 (autumn 2002): 134. At St. Katharine's Lodge he made a "very charming" Italianate garden. Evelyn Cecil, *London Parks and Gardens* (London: Archibald Constable & Co, 1907).

89 DTJ 5928, June 27, 1878.

90 March 4, 1880, Trinity College Myers, 7(19)-1.

91 FM diary, Trinity College Myers 14/1. William Marshall (1849–1921) was the father of Bloomsbury diarist Frances Partridge and, like Myers, a cousin of Annie Marshall. He had in 1876 designed an extension to Charles Darwin's home, Down House in Kent. His other Cambridge buildings are the University real tennis court and clubhouse in Grange Road (1890) and the Perse School (1893–1900).

92 EM to FM, [?] March 29, 1883, Trinity College Myers, 1883. Broadlands: DTJ 5930, October 9,10, 1880. Georgina Cowper-Temple (1821?–1901) became Lady Mount-Temple when her husband was raised to the peerage in 1880.

93 Watts 1910.

94 "The Grosvenor Gallery," *The Times*, April 25, 1885, issue 31430. "My Note Book," *Art Amateur* 13, no. 4 (September 1885): 66.

[95] Bockrath 2021 states: "The x-radiograph […] exhibits an extensive patch of density in the area of the red flowers behind the sitter's hair on the left and in front of her face to the right […] which does not correspond exactly to the distribution of the red flowers […]. The density here appears to come mainly from an extensive patch of roughly applied pale gray paint that lies under the red flowers and that does not relate to the upper design. This patch lends texture to the overlying layer of brown paint that comprises the hair behind the sitter's neck."

[96] Although the two were no longer living together, the divorce between Terry and Watts was not finalized until 1877.

[97] Autograph letter, GFW to DT, Little Holland House, October 23, 1879.

[98] DTJ 5926, March 20, 1876. *Eve Tempted*, Watts Gallery COMWG142, begun around 1868.

[99] DTJ 5928, June 22, 1878.

[100] March 12, 1880, Trinity College Myers, 7/23.

[101] *Fragments of Inner Life: An Autobiographical Sketch by Frederic W. H. Myers* (London: Society for Psychical Research, 1961), 11. Praxilla was a Greek woman lyric poet of the 5th century BC.

[102] "Gainsborough": DTJ 5924, August 27, 1874. Mrs. E. I. Barrington, *Catalogue of Paintings by G F Watts, R.A., […] on Exhibition at the Metropolitan Museum of Art, New York* (New York: Metropolitan Museum of Art, 1884–85), 4.

[103] Bockrath 2021.

[104] See Lynn Alexander, *Women, Work, and Representation. Needlewomen in Victorian Art and Literature* (Athens: Ohio University Press, 2003).

[105] The gift was in exchange for a portrait Watts had made of Millais in 1871. Leonée and Richard Ormond, *G. F. Watts: The Hall of Fame: Portraits of His Famous Contemporaries* (Compton: Watts Gallery, 2012), 60.

[106] GFW to J. E. Millais, July 19, 1876, quoted in J. G. Millais, *The Life and Letters of Sir John Everett Millais* (London: Methuen, 1899), vol. II, 83. In 1887, according to Mary Watts's diary, it was hanging in the dining room at Little Holland House. Desna Greenhow, ed., *The Diary of Mary Watts 1887–1904* (London: Lund Humphries in association with Watts Gallery, 2016), 38.

[107] ET to Brinsley Marlay, Hotel France et Bath, Paris, January 13, 1880. My 3541 (1), Marlay Collection.

[108] January 19, 1880, Trinity College Myers, 3/75, quoted in James Gregory, *Reformers, Patrons, and Philanthropists: The Cowper-Temples and High Politics in Victorian Britain* (London: Tauris Academic Studies, 2010), 156–57.

[109] Watts 1910, 156.

[110] M. S. Watts to D. C. Thomson, June 5, 1906. Copy of typewritten letter forwarded by Thomson to Bancroft, Samuel and Mary R. Bancroft Pre-Raphaelite Manuscript Collection, Delaware Art Museum, Box 12. (Hereafter Bancroft Collection). Mary Watts simply records Agnew's as the owners in Watts 1910.

[111] Samuel Bancroft to D. Croal Thomson of Thomas Agnew & Sons, June 22, 1906. Typewritten letter, Bancroft Collection, Box 12.

[112] Bancroft to Thomson, June 22, 1906.

[113] Bockrath 2021.

[114] Gould, *G.F. Watts. The Last Great Victorian*, 2004, 125, 150.

[115] DTJ 5929, November 19, 1879.

[116] FM to Henry Sidgwick, January 1, 1879 [1880],Trinity College Myers, 12/151. Henner: DTJ 5929, January 11, 1880, January 20, 1880. The whereabouts of this portrait, a gift from Henner to Eveleen, and left by her in her will to her son Harold, are unknown.

[117] Trinity College Myers, 14/1. Gertrude wrote to Marlay from Paris on January 5, 1880, to inform him of Eveleen's engagement. My 3539, Marlay Collection. Myers wrote to George Eliot to tell her of his engagement on January 9, 1880. *The Journals of George Eliot*, ed. Margaret Harris and Judith Johnston (Cambridge: Cambridge University Press, 1998), 195.

[118] ET to FM, January 19 and 20, 1880, Trinity College Myers, 6/2. Augustin Aimé Joseph Le Jeune, who had photographed the French Imperial family and the British Royal Family in the 1860s and 1870s, sold his rue St Honoré and rue de Rivoli studios in 1874 and 1873 respectively, but his successors continued to trade under his name.

[119] ET to FM, January 28, 1880, Trinity College Myers, 6/8. Henry Maull (1829–1914) was in partnership with John Fox (1832–1907) from 1879 to 1885. The firm photographed many of the most important people of the day.

[120] ET to FM, January 19, 1880, Trinity College Myers, 6/2.

[121] "We do not care for his way of painting, or his pictures; he wanted me to sit to him, in your favourite hat, but I am not going to." ET to FM, January 30, 1880, Trinity College Myers, 6/9(1).

[122] Mary Reed Bobbitt, *With Dearest Love to All: The Life and Letters of Lady Jebb* (London: Faber and Faber, 1960), 155. When Caroline Jebb did finally meet Eveleen she was not impressed, dubbing her a "bar-maid beauty." Letter to her sister, June 3, 1880, Bobbitt 1960, 159.

[123] Return from Paris: DTJ 5929.

[124] Trinity College Myers, 25/3.

[125] Trinity College Myers, 14/1. My particular thanks to James Kirwan for checking this transcription. Arthur Myers was a spiritual researcher like his brother and also a physician.

[126] Bockrath 2021.

[127] C. B. Marlay to GT, January 12, 1880. My3540, Marlay Collection.

[128] "Mrs. Frederic Myers. Camera Portraits," *The Times*, March 13, 1937.

[129] Bockrath 2021.

[130] GFW to ET, January 15, 1880. Trinity College Myers, 25/4.

[131] M. S. Watts 1912.

[132] Athena Vrettos, "Displaced Memories in Victorian Fiction and Psychology," *Victorian Studies* 49, no. 2 (winter 2007), 199–207, discusses with reference to Myers's writing the late Victorian belief that an object can become a site for thought transference.

[133] "Insidious nature," Caroline Jebb to her sister, June 20, 1878, quoted in Bobbitt 1960, 141.

[134] GFW to FM, January 12, 1882. Trinity College Myers, 4/133.

[135] Written, according to his diary, on January 12 and 13, 1882. Repr. in FM, *The Renewal of Youth and Other Poems* (1882) and in Eveleen Myers, ed., *Collected Poems [...] by Frederic W. H. Myers* (1921).

[136] GFW to EM, February 3, 1882. Trinity College Myers, 25/5(1).

[137] Barbara Bryant, "G. F. Watts and the Symbolist Vision," in *The Age of Rossetti, Burne-Jones & Watts. Symbolism in Britain 1860–1910*, ed. Andrew Wilton and Robert Upstone (London: Tate Gallery Publishing, 1997), 292, 56n.

[138] Roger Luckhurst, *The Invention of Telepathy 1870–1901* (Oxford: University Press, 2002), 56.

[139] DTJ 5926, September 16, 1876.

[140] M. S. Watts 1912, vol. I, 116–17.

[141] Watts, 1912, 115.

[142] "Ross A. Slotten, *The Heretic in Darwin's Court. The Life of Alfred Russel Wallace* (New York: Columbia University Press, 2004), 343.

[143] DTJ 5926, November 30, 1876. John Maskelyne (1839–1917) performed at the Egyptian Hall 1873–1904. *Modern Spiritualism: A Short Account of its Rise and Progress, with Some Exposures of So-Called Spirit Media* (1875). The author describes himself on the title page as "Illusionist and Anti-Spiritualist." See also Hamilton 2009, 93, 96, 98, 163, 218–19.

[144] "Talk on spirits:" [March] 30, [1880]; Maskelyne: [July] 12 [1880], FM Diary, Trinity College Myers, 14/1.

[145] FM Diary, March 16, 1878, October 25, 1878, and January 23, 1879, Trinity College Myers 14/1. Marian (Maidie or Mady) Huxley (1859–1887), Dolly's great friend from the Slade. The friendship did not survive Mady's marriage to portrait painter John Collier in 1879, for Dolly herself was in love with him.

[146] DTJ 5929, February 16, 1880.

[147] DTJ 5929, February 16, 1880. Responding in 1871 to a request from the London Dialectical Society that he should join a committee to investigate spiritualism Huxley had replied, "The only case of "Spiritualism" I have had the opportunity of examining into for myself, was as gross an imposture as ever came under my notice. But supposing the phenomena to be genuine—they do not interest me." Quoted in Leonard Huxley, *The Life and Letters of Thomas Henry Huxley* (Cambridge: Cambridge University Press, 2012), 144.

[148] DTJ 5929, February 16, 1880. Huxley advised his daughter Marian to consult Charcot in Paris during her psychiatric illness of 1887. Ronald W. Clark, *The Huxleys* (London: Heinemann, 1968), 109.

[149] See Mary Walker, "Between Fiction and Madness: "The Relationship of Women to the Supernatural in Late Victorian Britain," in Lynda L. Coon, Katherine J. Haldane, and Elisabeth W. Sommer, *That Gentle Strength: Historical Perspectives on Women in Christianity* (Charlottesville: University of Virginia Press, 1990), 235–36. Rita McWilliams-Tullberg, *Women at Cambridge: A Men's University—Though of a Mixed Type* (London: Victor Gollancz Ltd, 1975), 51–59

[150] FM Diary, Trinity College Myers, 14/1.

[151] FM, *Science and a Future Life: With Other Essays* (London: Macmillan, 1893), 63–64.

[152] Trinity College Myers, 26/63/48–77, quoted in Hamilton 2009, 208.

[153] FM Diary, entries for July 14 and 18, 1878, Trinity College Myers 14/1.

[154] N. F., "Mrs. F. W. H. Myers' Recollections," in *Light: A Journal of Psychical, Occult, and Mystical Research* 54 (June 1, 1934), 332.

[155] Eveleen as medium: Hamilton 2009, 284.

[156] N.F. 1934, 332.

[157] ET to FM, January 28, 1880, Trinity College Myers, 6/8(1).

[158] FM to EM, June 29, 1880, Trinity College Myers, 7/25.

[159] FM to EM, October 11, 1884, Trinity College Myers, 7/162.

[160] FM to EM, October 13, 1884, Trinity College Myers, 7/163.

[161] EM to FM, August 17, 1884, Trinity College Myers, 6/76. Richmond Terrace; March 29, 1885, Trinity College Myers, 29/85.

[162] FM to EM, Wednesday, October 1884, Trinity College Myers, 7/159.

[163] DTJ 5934, December 20, 1884.

[164] March 29, 1885, Trinity College Myers, 29/85.

[165] An example of Eveleen's philanthropic work is given in a letter by Myers to "Sally," dated January 6, 1898. He states that Eveleen had recently caught diphtheria and almost died as result of visiting some poor people's homes for the Society for the Prevention of Cruelty to Children. The philanthropic side of psychical research is discussed in *The Ashgate Research Companion to Nineteenth-Century Spiritualism and the Occult*, ed. Tatiana Kontou and Sarah Willburn (Farnham: Ashgate, 2012), 6–7.

[166] N.F. 1934, 332.

[167] FM 1918, vol. II, 288.

[168] FM 1961, 5.

[169] See Hamilton 2009, 283-292.

[170] EM Commonplace Book, Trinity College Myers, 26/60.

[171] GFW to EM, February 3, 1882, Trinity College Myers 25/5(1).

[172] In contrast to his wife's effusiveness, Myers's only comment in his diary is "G. F. Watts calls." Trinity College Myers, 14/1.

[173] DTJ 5933, June 14, 1883.

[174] "List of contemporary portrait painters with E. & Dolly," November 26 [1883], FM Diary 1864–1900, Trinity College Myers, 14/3. Frank Holl (1845–1888).

[175] "6 painters voted for amongst painters as best 1888," FM Diary 1864–1900, Trinity College Myers, 14/3. Lawrence Alma-Tadema (1836–1912); Edward Burne-Jones (1832–1898); William Quiller Orchardson (1832–1910).

[176] FM, manuscript draft autobiography dated June 4, 1893; Watts reference dated June 3, [18]91. Trinity College Myers, 26/63.

[177] Myers 1961, 30.

[178] FM, proof sheets autobiography, dated May 16, 1900. Trinity College Myers, 18/76(1). John Couch Adams (1819–1892), Professor of Astronomy at Cambridge.

[179] "G. F. Watts, R.A.," *Journal of the Society for Psychical Research* 11 (1904), 268–69, reprinted in EM 1904, 115–16.

[180] EM to FM, June 26, 1899, Trinity College Myers, 6/246.

[181] He had been collecting "Pre-Raphaelite" works through Agnew's since 1892. Their label, slightly torn, remains on the back of the frame.

[182] Stock no. 9405, Thos. Agnew & Sons, Picture Stock Book 1898–1904, NGA27/1/1/9, National Gallery, London. The stock book records that Agnew's bought the work from Watts on May 22, 1900. https://www.nationalgallery.org.uk/research/research-centre/agnews-stock-books. Licensed for non-commercial use under a Creative Commons agreement.

[183] Chloe Ward, "England's Michelangelo in the Metropolitan Museum of Art: The G. F. Watts Exhibition, 1884–85." *Comparative American Studies* 14 (spring 2016), 62–75.

[184] See Jeffrey J. Kripal, *Authors of the Impossible: The Paranormal and the Sacred* (Chicago: University of Chicago Press, 2010), 39–40. Myers 1961, 37.

[185] " 'Yes' and 'No'—A Victorian Flashback. Sister on Art and Romance," *Star*, November 25, 1933.

[186] Samuel Bancroft to D. Croal Thomson of Thomas Agnew & Sons, June 22, 1906, typewritten letter, Bancroft Collection, Box 12. Croal Thomson (1855–1930) was a partner in Agnew's from 1898 to 1908 and editor of the *Art Journal* from 1892 to 1902.

[187] M. S. Watts to D. C. Thomson, Limnerslease, June 5, 1906, copy of typewritten letter, Bancroft Collection, Box 12.

[188] Rowland Elzea, *The Samuel and Mary R. Bancroft Jr. and Related Pre-Raphaelite Collections*. Rev. ed. (Wilmington: Delaware Art Museum, 1984), 182–83.

[189] NGA27/1/1/9 (1898–1904), 128, op. cit.

[190] DTJ 5929, October 27, 1879.

[191] The Edith Martineau picture, also known as *The Cello Player*, was bought by Bancroft in 1893 at the Chicago World's Fair and Exposition, sold after his death and was unlocated in 1997, see Rowland Elzea, "Samuel Bancroft: Pre-Raphaelite Collector," in *Collecting the Pre-Raphaelites: the Anglo-American Enchantment*, ed. Margaretta Frederick Watson (Aldershot: Ashgate, 1997), 29.

[192] Samuel Bancroft to Gerald Agnew, April 6, 1909, typewritten letter, Bancroft Collection, Box 12. Gerald Agnew (1882–1954) joined the firm in 1904 and was at the Manchester office, where Bancroft wrote to him, until World War I, retiring from the firm in 1952. Geoffrey Agnew and Thos. Agnew and Sons Ltd., *Agnew's, 1817–1967* (London: Bradbury Agnew Press, 1967), 45. For *The White Cockade*, see Elzea 1984, 76–77.

[193] DTJ 5924, August 18, 1874.

[194] Elzea 1997, 26.

[195] Margaretta S. Frederick, "Portrait of Eveleen Tennant [Jessamine] (later Mrs. F. W. H. Myers," in Stephen Wildman, et al, *Waking Dreams: The Art of the Pre-Raphaelites from the Delaware Art Museum* (Alexandria, VA: Art Services International, 2004), 274.

[196] Samuel Bancroft to D. Croal Thomson of Thomas Agnew & Sons, June 22, 1906, typewritten letter, Bancroft Collection, Box 12.

[197] D. Croal Thomson to Samuel Bancroft, June 8, 1906, typewritten letter, Bancroft Collection, Box 12.

[198] Samuel Bancroft to D. Croal Thomson, June 22, 1906, typewritten letter, Bancroft Collection, Box 12. Bancroft is reporting back to Thomson what the dealer had previously told him. Hollyer's photograph is at the Watts Gallery (COMWG2007.775), as are his photographs of Watts's other portrait of Eveleen (COMWG2007.790) and his portrait of Dolly (COMWG2007.711). Frederick Hollyer (1838–1933), artistic photographer whose reproductions of the painting and drawings of Burne-Jones, Rossetti, and Watts in particular did much to popularize their work. He was a member of the Linked Ring.

[199] *Fragments of Prose & Poetry by Frederic W. H. Myers*, ed. Eveleen Myers (London: Longmans Green, 1904), 205.

[200] His friendship with the Cambridge moral philosopher Henry Sidgwick had begun in 1869 over a shared interest in women's higher education and Rossetti's sonnets. A[rthur] S[idgwick], and E[leanor] M[ary] S[idgwick], *Henry Sidgwick: A Memoir* (London: Macmillan & Co, 1906), 196, 215, 227, 232.

[201] Trinity College Myers, 14/1.

[202] FM, "Rossetti and the Religion of Beauty," *Cornhill Magazine* 47 (February 1883), 213–24.

[203] In a letter to Eveleen of October 11, 1884, Myers, begging her to be his companion in psychical research, wrote: "I want to feel as Rossetti says 'the breath of kindred plumes against my feet.'" Trinity College Myers 7/162.

[204] Myers 1885, 320.

[205] "exclusiveness," Myers 1961, 29. "highest things," Myers 1885, 334.

[206] R. Buchanan, "The Fleshly School of Poetry: The Poetry of Mr. D. G. Rossetti," *Contemporary Review* 18 (October 1871): 332–50. See also Barbara Bryant, "G. F. Watts and the Symbolist Vision," in Wilton and Upstone 1997, 69–70. James Ashcroft Noble's paper "The Sonnet in England," *Contemporary Review* (September 1880), made a similar point two years before Myers and gratified Rossetti before his death. Noble argued that because Rossetti's sonnets were "purely artistic," they should be exempted from "irritating pseudo-ethical controversies."

[207] We know that Myers was interested in the subject of witches. With characteristic sympathy for the specifics of female experience he pointed out, for example, that the fact witches believed their hallucinations to be true was sufficient to make them worthy of serious scientific investigation. FM, *Human Personality and Its Survival of Bodily Death* (London: Longmans Green, 1918), vol. 1, 4–5. See also "Note on Witchcraft" in Edmund Gurney, FM and Frank Podmore, *Phantasms of the Living* (London: Society for Psychical Research and Trübner and Co, 1886), vol. I, 172–85.

[208] See the discussion of *Lady Lilith* and *Sibylla Palmifera* in Julian Treuherz, Elizabeth Prettejohn, and Edwin Becker, *Dante Gabriel Rossetti* (London: Thames and Hudson, 2003), 191–93.

[209] Myers 1885, 326.

[210] Mrs. Russell Barrington, *G. F. Watts: Reminiscences* (London: George Allen, 1905), 2.

[211] Myers 1885, 326, 319.

[212] "The Photographs of the Month." Review of Reviews, ed. W. T. Stead [July? 1890], 189–92. In a letter of July 22, 1891, to FM she writes of a "long [...] glowing kind" article on her photographs in a Swiss newspaper, Trinity College Myers, 6/179.

[213] EM to FM, January 22, 1891, Trinity College Myers, 6/169.

[214] Belloc 1896, 762.

[215] "The head [...] is in strict profile, and has a pathetic expression, as of a vigorous old age battling undismayed but conscious with the inroads of time. The eye—as so often happens in photography—comes too small, besides being veiled by its fleshy integuments, yet has a very earnest and "deep-down" expression. The mouth has also suffered, as the contour of moustache and beard offers a delusive appearance of a very long and straight upper lip." W. M. Rossetti, "Portraits of Robert Browning. III.," *Magazine of Art*, 1890, 264–65. Lord Rayleigh, another of Eveleen's sitters, criticized her overuse of retouching. Trinity College Myers, 19/39.

[216] M. H. Spielmann, *Millais and His Works, with Special Reference to the Exhibition at the Royal Academy 1898* (Edinburgh: William Blackwood and Sons, 1898), 65.

[217] *Magazine of Art*, 1891, 310–16. Spielmann had hoped to include a third photograph, of Adelaide Passingham, but Eveleen seems to have found it too complicated to ask her for permission and easier to use two of her son Harold instead. EM to FM, January 22, 1891, Trinity College Myers, 6/169. Two of Eveleen's photographs of Miss Passingham are now in the NPG, Ax36315 and Ax68631.

[218] P. H. Emerson, quoted in Nancy Newhall, *P. H. Emerson, The Fight for Photography as a Fine Art* (New York: Aperture, 1975), 75.

[219] London: the author, 1890.

[220] EM to FM, July 17, 1891, Trinity College Myers, 6/177.

221 Liz Rideal, *Mirror Mirror: Self-Portraits by Women Artists* (London: National Portrait Gallery, 2001), 50. Margaret F. Harker, "Emerson and the Linked Ring," in *Life and Landscape: P. H. Emerson, Art and Photography in East Anglia 1885–1900*, ed. Neil McWilliam and Veronica Sekules (Norwich: Sainsbury Centre for Visual Arts, University of East Anglia, 1986), 64–68. Eveleen is not mentioned in Harker's *The Linked Ring: The Secession Movement in Photography in Britain, 1892–1910* (London: Heinemann, 1979).

222 Her two portrait studies of him are at the NPG, x19819 and x19820 and a third at the University of Bristol Library, Special Collections [DM375/1]. For Myers and Symonds see Amber K. Regis, *The Memoirs of John Addington Symonds: A Critical Edition* (London: Palgrave Macmillan, 2016).

223 John Addington Symonds, "Mrs. F. W. H. Myers," *Sun Artists*, no. 7 (April 1891), 54. W. A. Boord's *Sun Artists* was published by Kegan Paul, a friend of the Tennants. An article by Emerson on Julia Margaret Cameron had appeared in it the previous year.

224 Belloc 1896, 770.

225 Meaghan Clarke, "(Re)Envisioning New Women. Eveleen Myers and Gertrude Campbell" in *Fashionability, Exhibition Culture, and Gender Politics: Fair Women* (London: Routledge, 2020), 88–105; Judy Oberhausen and Nic Peeters, "Eveleen Myers (1856–1937): Portraying Beauty; The Rediscovery of a Late-Victorian Aesthetic Photographer," *British Art Journal* 17, no. 1 (spring 2016), 94–102.

226 EM to FM 1 August 1889, Trinity College Myers, 6/152. Eveleen told Marie Belloc in 1896 that she preferred to dress her female sitters in pale yellow or pink as black came across as too dark and white too glaring. Belloc 1896, 769.

227 EM, "Léonie I" and "Léonie II", NPG Ax68618 and Ax68564, published in W. T. Stead, ed. "Real Ghost Stories," *Review of Reviews* (December 1891), 11ff.

228 William James, "Frederic Myers's Service to Psychology," *Proceedings of the Society for Psychical Research 17* (1903), 13.

229 N. F. 1934, 332.

230 Piper 1919, 53.

231 Henry James to FM, November 18, 1890, Trinity College Myers, 2/137.

232 Leon Edel, ed., *The Ghostly Tales of Henry James* (New Brunswick, NJ: Rutgers University Press, 1948), xii.

233 Hamilton 2009, 205.

234 Hamilton 2009, 287–89. See also G. H. Bantock, *L. H. Myers. A Critical Study* (London: University College and Jonathan Cape, 1956), 138.

235 Myers 1918, vol. 2, 394.

236 William H. Brock, *William Crookes (1832–1919) and the Commercialization of Science* (Aldershot: Ashgate, 2008), 188ff.

237 M. J. G. Cattermole and A. F. Wolfe, *Horace Darwin's Shop: A History of the Cambridge Scientific Instrument Company 1878 to 1968* (Bristol: Adam Hilger, 1987). At the time of Eveleen's contact in St Tibb's Row, off Downing Street.

238 Joseph John Thomson, *Recollections and Reflections* (New York: Macmillan, 1937), 285, quoted in Joseph Viscomi, "Two Fake Blakes Revisited; One Dew-Smith Revealed," in *Blake in Our Time: Essays in Honour of G. E. Bentley, Jr.*, ed. Karen Mulhallen, (Toronto: University of Toronto Press, 2010), 54.

[239] A letter from Dew-Smith to Eveleen written just before his marriage to Alice Lloyd in 1895 surprised her with its declaration that the hours passed in her company were the most pleasant he had ever spent. She wrote at the foot of the letter: "I don't know if he is as happy as he ought to be. He only lunched 3 or 4 times here with us when he first helped me to photograph. I did not know he had liked it." She scratched out the last two lines of what he had written lest they incriminate him. Albert Dew-Smith to EM, October 25, 1895, Trinity College Myers, 22/42.

[240] FM to ET, January 21, 1880, Trinity College Myers 7/10; F. W. H. Myers, "Tennyson as Prophet," *Nineteenth Century* 25 (March 1889): 381–96. See Alison Chapman, "'A Poet Never Sees a Ghost': Photography and Trance in Tennyson's Enoch Arden and Julia Margaret Cameron's Photography," *Victorian Poetry* 41, no. 1 (spring 2003): 47–71.

[241] Oscar Wilde, 'The Canterville Ghost," in *The Canterville Ghost, The Happy Prince, and Other Stories* (London: Penguin Books, 2010), 196, 208.

[242] Napoleon's brother Oliver set up business in England as Sarony and Co and photographed Myers himself in about 1873. NPG Ax58318.

[243] Myers 1961, 5.

[244] EM to FM, January 24, 1892, Trinity College Myers, 6/188.

[245] M. H. Spielmann, "Notes on the Pictures Exhibited at the Royal Academy, 1898" in Spielmann 1898, 143. Lillie Langtry is the other female sitter of whom he may have been thinking. Millais, *A Jersey Lily* (1877–78, Jersey Museums Service); Watts, *The Dean's Daughter (Lillie Langtry)* (1879–80, Watts Gallery Trust). Dolly describes seeing "two unfinished heads of Mrs Langtry" at Watts's studio on October 30, 1879. DTJ 5929.

[246] Henry James, *The Portrait of a Lady* (London: Macmillan and Co., 1881), vol. I, 55.

[247] James 1881, 57.

[248] Samuel Bancroft to D. Croal Thomson of Thomas Agnew & Sons, June 22, 1906, typewritten letter, Bancroft Collection, Box 12.

[249] Rowland Elzea in Watson 1997, 26, 30. There is an 1880 photograph in Bancroft's collection of John Bright with J. E. Millais. DAM_SB_PHO_34_10.

[250] Dorothy became Lady Stanley when her husband was made a knight grand cross in the Order of the Bath in 1899. She continued to use the title after his death and her remarriage.

BIBLIOGRAPHY

Agnew, Geoffrey, and Thos. Agnew and Sons Ltd. *Agnew's, 1817–1967*. London: Bradbury Agnew Press, 1967.

Alexander, Lynn. *Women, Work, and Representation: Needlewomen in Victorian Art and Literature*. Athens: Ohio University Press, 2003.

Allen, Gay Wilson. *William James: A Biography*. London: Rupert Hart-Davis, 1967.

Anesko, Michael, and Greg W. Zacharias, eds. The Complete Letters of Henry James, 1883–1884. 2 vols. Lincoln: University of Nebraska Press, 2019.

Armstrong, Margaret. *Linen and Liturgy: The Story of the Marshall Family and the Parish Church of Keswick St. John*. Keswick: Peel Wyke Publications, 2002.

Barrington, Mrs. E. I. [Elizabeth Isabelle Barrington]. *Catalogue of Paintings by G. F. Watts, R.A. [...] on Exhibition at the Metropolitan Museum of Art*, New York. New York: Metropolitan Museum of Art, 1884–85.

———. Barrington, Mrs. Russell [Elizabeth Isabelle Barrington]. *G.F. Watts: Reminiscences*. London: George Allen, 1905.

Beer, John. *Providence and Love: Studies in Wordsworth, Channing, Myers, George Eliot, and Ruskin*. Oxford: Clarendon Press, 1998.

———. *Post-Romantic Consciousness: Dickens to Plath*. Basingstoke: Palgrave Macmillan, 2003.

Belloc, Marie A. "An Interview with Mrs. F. W. H. Myers." *The Woman at Home, Annie S. Swan's Magazine* (June 1896): 761–70.

Bills, Mark, and Barbara Bryant. *G. F. Watts, Victorian Visionary; Highlights from the Watts Gallery Collection*. New Haven: Yale University Press in association with Watts Gallery Compton, 2008. Published in conjunction with an exhibition of the same name at the Guildhall Art Gallery, London, November 11, 2008–April 26, 2009.

Blum, Deborah. *Ghost Hunters: William James and the Search for Scientific Proof of Life After Death*. London: Century, 2007.

Bobbitt, Mary Reed. *With Dearest Love to All: The Life and Letters of Lady Jebb*. London: Faber and Faber, 1960.

Bond, R. Warwick. *The Marlay Letters 1778–1820*. London: Constable, 1937.

Breward, Christopher, Edwina Ehrman, and Caroline Evans. *The London Look: Fashion from Street to Catwalk*. New Haven: Yale University Press in association with the Museum of London, 2004.

Brock, William H. *William Crookes (1832–1919) and the Commercialization of Science*. Aldershot: Ashgate, 2008.

Bryant, Barbara. G. F. Watts Portraits. *Fame & Beauty in Victorian Society*. London: National Portrait Gallery, 2004. Published in conjunction with an exhibition of the same name at the National Portrait Gallery, London, October 14 2004–January 9, 2009.

———. *G. F. Watts in Kensington: Little Holland House and Gallery*. Compton: Watts Gallery, 2009.

Buchanan, R. "The Fleshly School of Poetry: The Poetry of Mr. D. G. Rossetti." *Contemporary Review* 18 (October 1871): 332–50.

Burn, Lucilla. *The Fitzwilliam Museum: A History*. London: Philip Wilson Publishers, 2016.

Casteras, Susan P. *English Pre-Raphaelitism and Its Reception in America in the Nineteenth Century*. London: Associated University Presses, 1990.

Cattermole, M. J. G., and A. F. Wolfe. *Horace Darwin's Shop: A History of the Cambridge Scientific Instrument Company 1878 to 1968*. Bristol: Adam Hilger, 1987.

Cecil, Evelyn. *London Parks and Gardens*. London: Archibald Constable & Co, 1907.

Chapman, Alison. "'A Poet Never Sees a Ghost': Photography and Trance in Tennyson's *Enoch Arden* and Julia Margaret Cameron's Photography." *Victorian Poetry* 41, no. 1 (spring 2003): 47–71. https://doi.org/10.1353/vp.2003.0008.

Clark, Ronald W. *The Huxleys*. London: Heinemann, 1968.

Clarke, Meaghan. *Fashionability, Exhibition Culture, and Gender Politics: Fair Women*. London: Routledge, 2020.

Coleman, Elizabeth Ann. *The Opulent Era: Fashions of Worth, Doucet and Pingat*. London: Thames and Hudson, 1989.

Coon, Lynda L., Katherine J. Haldane, and Elisabeth W. Sommer. *That Gentle Strength: Historical Perspectives on Women in Christianity*. Charlottesville: University of Virginia Press, 1990.

Dakers, Caroline. *The Holland Park Circle: Artists and Victorian Society*. New Haven: Yale University Press, 1999.

Drake, John, and Charles Malyon. "Leckhampton House and Garden." *Cambridgeshire Gardens Trust Newsletter* 19 (September 2005).

Durand-Gréville, Emile. *Entretiens de J-J Henner, Notes Prises par Emile Durand-Gréville, après ses conversations avec J-J Henner (1878–1888)*. Paris: Librairie Alphonse Lemerre, 1925.

Edel, Leon, ed. *The Ghostly Tales of Henry James*. New Brunswick, NJ: Rutgers University Press, 1948.

———. *Henry James: The Conquest of London 1870–1883*. London: Rupert Hart-Davis, 1962.

Edel, Leon, and Lyall H. Powers, eds. *The Complete Notebooks of Henry James*. Oxford: Oxford University Press, 1987.

Elzea, Rowland. *The Samuel and Mary R. Bancroft Jr. and Related Pre-Raphaelite Collections*. Rev. ed. Wilmington: Delaware Art Museum, 1984.

———. "Samuel Bancroft: Pre-Raphaelite Collector." In *Collecting the Pre-Raphaelites: the Anglo-American Enchantment*, edited by Margaretta Frederick Watson, 25–31. Aldershot: Ashgate, 1997.

Emerson, P. H. "The Artistic Aspects of Figure Photography." *Magazine of Art* (1891): 310–16.

F., N. "Mrs. F. W. H. Myers' Recollections." In *Light: A Journal of Psychical, Occult, and Mystical Research* 54 (June 1, 1934): 332.

Flint, Kate. *The Victorians and the Visual Imagination*. Cambridge: Cambridge University Press, 2000.

Gauld, Alan. *The Founders of Psychical Research*. London: Routledge & Kegan Paul, 1968.

Gitter, Elisabeth G. "The Power of Women's Hair in the Victorian Imagination." *Publications of the Modern Language Association of America* 99, no. 5 (October 1984): 936–54. https://doi.org/10.2307/462145.

Goodison, N. W., and Denys Sutton. "French, German Spanish." Vol. 1 of *Catalogue of Paintings*. Cambridge: Syndics of the Fitzwilliam Museum, Cambridge, 1960.

Gould, Veronica Franklin. *G. F. Watts: The Last Great Victorian*. New Haven: Yale University Press for the Paul Mellon Centre for Studies in British Art, 2004.

———, ed. *The Vision of G. F. Watts OM RA (1817–1904)*. Trustees of the Watts Gallery for the Watts Centenary Exhibition, 2004. Published in conjunction with the Watts Centenary Exhibition at the Watts Gallery, Compton, July 2–October 31, 2004.

Greenhow, Desna, ed. *The Diary of Mary Watts 1887–1904: Victorian Progressive and Artistic Visionary*. London: Lund Humphries, in association with the Watts Gallery, 2016.

Gregory, James. *Reformers, Patrons, and Philanthropists: The Cowper-Temples and High Politics in Victorian Britain*. London: Tauris Academic Studies, 2010.

Gurney, Edmund, Frederic W. H. Myers, and Frank Podmore. *Phantasms of the Living*. 2 vols. London: Society for Psychical Research and Trübner, 1886.

Hall, Trevor H. *The Spiritualists*. London: Gerald Duckworth, 1962.

Hamilton, Trevor. *Immortal Longings, F. W. H. Myers and the Victorian Search for Life after Death*. Exeter: Imprint Academic, 2009.

Harker, Margaret. *The Linked Ring: The Secession Movement in Photography in Britain, 1892–1910*. London: Heinemann, 1979.

Harris, Beth, ed. *Famine and Fashion: Needlewomen in the Nineteenth Century*. Aldershot: Ashgate, 2005.

Harris, Margaret, and Judith Johnston, eds. *The Journals of George Eliot*. Cambridge: Cambridge University Press, 1998.

Haye, Amy de la, and Valerie D. Mendes. *The House of Worth: Portrait of an Archive*. London: V&A Publishing, 2014.

Horne, Philip, ed. *Henry James: A Life in Letters*. London: Penguin Books, 1999.

Huxley, Leonard. *The Life and Letters of Thomas Henry Huxley*. Cambridge: Cambridge University Press, 2012.

Jacobi, Carol, and Hope Kingsley. *Painting with Light: Art and Photography from the Pre-Raphaelites to the Modern Age*. London: Tate Publishing, 2016. Published in conjunction with the exhibition of the same name at Tate Britain, London, May 11–September 25, 2016.

James, Henry. *The Portrait of a Lady*. 3 vols. London: Macmillan, 1881.

———. *The Bostonians*. London: Penguin Books, 2000.

James, William. "Frederic Myers's Service to Psychology." *Proceedings of the Society for Psychical Research* 17 (1903): 13–23.

Jolly, Martyn. *Faces of the Living Dead: The Belief in Spirit Photography*. London: British Library, 2006.

Kaplan, Fred. *Henry James: The Imagination of Genius, A Biography*. London: Hodder & Stoughton, 1992.

Kern, Stephen. *Eyes of Love: The Gaze in English and French Paintings and Novels, 1840–1900*. London: Reaktion Books, 1996.

Kerr, Howard. *Mediums and Spirit-Rappers and Roaring Radicals: Spiritualism in American Literature 1850–1900*. Chicago: University of Illinois Press, 1972.

Keynes, Margaret. *A House by the River: Newnham Grange to Darwin College*. Cambridge: privately printed, 1984.

Kontou, Tatiana, and Sarah Willburn, eds. *The Ashgate Research Companion to Nineteenth-Century Spiritualism and the Occult*. Farnham: Ashgate, 2012.

Kripal, Jeffrey J. *Authors of the Impossible: The Paranormal and the Sacred*. Chicago: University of Chicago Press, 2010.

Lannoy, Isabelle de. "Jean-Jacques Henner et 'l'atelier des dames'. 'Des têtes, des morceaux seulement?'" In Françoise Sarret et al., *Marie Petiet: être femme peintre au 19e siècle*. Milan: Silvano Editoriale, 2014. Published in conjunction with the exhibition of the same name at Musée Petiet, Limoux, France, April 1–June 20, 2014.

Lowndes, Mrs. Belloc. *The Merry Wives of Westminster*. London: Macmillan, 1946.

Luckhurst, Roger. *The Invention of Telepathy 1870–1901*. Oxford: University Press, 2002.

Lustig, T. J. *Henry James and the Ghostly*. Cambridge: Cambridge University Press, 1994.

Lutyens, Mary, ed. *Effie in Venice: Unpublished Letters of Mrs. John Ruskin Written from Venice between 1849 and 1852*. London: Pallas Editions, 1999.

Mancoff, Debra N. ed. *Flora Symbolica: Flowers in Pre-Raphaelite Art*. New York: Prestel, 2003.

Maskelyne, John. *Modern Spiritualism: A Short Account of Its Rise and Progress, with Some Exposures of So-Called Spirit Media*. London: for the author by Frederick Warne and Co., 1875.

McCorristine, Shane. *Spectres of the Self: Thinking about Ghosts and Ghost-Seeing in England 1750–1920*. Cambridge: Cambridge University Press, 2010.

McWilliam, Neil, and Veronica Sekules, eds. *Life and Landscape: P. H. Emerson, Art and Photography in East Anglia 1885–1900*. Norwich: Sainsbury Centre for Visual Arts, University of East Anglia, 1986. Published in conjunction with the exhibition of the same name at the Sainsbury Centre, Norwich, July 28–October 26, 1986.

McWilliams-Tullberg, Rita. *Women at Cambridge: A Men's University—Though of a Mixed Type*. London: Victor Gollancz, 1975.

Millais, J. G. *The Life and Letters of Sir John Everett Millais*. 2 vols. London: Methuen, 1899.

Myers, Eveleen, ed. *Fragments of Prose & Poetry by Frederic W. H. Myers*. London: Longmans, Green, 1904.

———. *Collected Poems with Autobiographical and Critical Fragments by Frederic W. H. Myers*. London: Macmillan, 1921.

———. "Mrs. F. W. H. Myers. Amateur Photographer and Artist." *Cambridge Graphic* (November 1900): 4.

Myers, F. W. H. *The Renewal of Youth and Other Poems*. London: Macmillan, 1882.

———. "Rossetti and the Religion of Beauty." *Cornhill Magazine* 47 (February 1883): 213–24.

———. *Essays. Modern*. 2nd ed. London: Macmillan, 1885.

———. "Human Personality in the light of Hypnotic Suggestion." *Proceedings of the Society for Psychical Research* 4 (1885): 1–24.

———. "Tennyson as Prophet." *Nineteenth Century* 25 (March 1889): 381–96.

———. *Science and a Future Life: With Other Essays*. London: Macmillan, 1893.

———. *Human Personality and Its Survival of Bodily Death*. 2 vols. London: Longmans Green, 1918.

———. *Fragments of Inner Life: An Autobiographical Sketch by Frederic W. H. Myers*. London: Society for Psychical Research, 1961.

Newhall, Nancy. *P. H. Emerson: The Fight for Photography as a Fine Art*. New York: Aperture, c. 1975.

Noble, James Ashcroft. "The Sonnet in England." *Contemporary Review* (September 1880); repr. in *The Sonnet in England, and Other Essays*. London: Elkin Mathews and John Lane, 1893.

Oberhausen, Judy, and Nic Peeters, "Eveleen Myers (1856–1937): Portraying Beauty; The Rediscovery of a Late-Victorian Aesthetic Photographer." *British Art Journal* 17, no. 1 (spring 2016): 94–102.

Oppenheim, Janet. *Spiritualism and Psychical Research in England, 1850–1914*. Cambridge: Cambridge University Press, 1985.

Ormond, Leonée, and Richard Ormond. *G. F. Watts: The Hall of Fame: Portraits of His Famous Contemporaries*. Compton: Watts Gallery, 2012. Published in conjunction with an exhibition of the same name at the Watts Gallery, February 7–June 3 2012.

Paradis, James, and Thomas Postlewait. *Victorian Science and Victorian Values: Literary Perspectives*. New York: New York Academy of Sciences, 1981.

Pepper, Terence. *Edwardian Women Photographers: Eveleen Myers, Alice Hughes, Christina Broom, and Olive Edis*. London: National Portrait Gallery, 1994. Published in conjunction with an exhibition of the same name at the National Portrait Gallery, London, July 8–September 25, 1994.

Piper, Alta L. *The Life and Work of Mrs. Piper.* London: Kegan Paul, Trench, Trubner, 1919.

Pohlmann, Ulrich. commissariat général, Helen Adkins et al. *Qui a peur des femmes photographes? 1839–1945*. Paris: Musées d'Orsay et de l'Orangerie, Éditions Hazan, 2015. Published in conjunction with an exhibition of the same name at the Musée d'Orsay, Paris, October 14, 2015–January 24, 2016.

Postle, Martin, and William Vaughan. *The Artist's Model: From Etty to Spencer.* London: Merrell Holberton Publishers, c. 1999.

Prettejohn, Elizabeth, ed. *After the Pre-Raphaelites; Art and Aestheticism in Victorian England.* Manchester: Manchester University Press, c. 1999.

Prodger, Phillip. *Victorian Giants: The Birth of Art Photography.* London: National Portrait Gallery, 2018.

Regis, Amber K. *The Memoirs of John Addington Symonds: A Critical Edition.* London: Palgrave Macmillan, 2016.

Rideal, Liz. *Mirror Mirror: Self-Portraits by Women Artists.* London: National Portrait Gallery, 2001. Published in conjunction with an exhibition of the same name at the National Portrait Gallery, October 24, 2001–February 24, 2002.

Ritchie, Hester, ed. *Letters of Anne Thackeray Ritchie.* London: John Murray, 1924.

Rosenfeld, Jason, and Alison Smith. *Millais.* London: Tate Publishing, 2007. Published in conjunction with the exhibition *Millais* at Tate Britain, London, September 26, 2007 - 13 January, 2008.

Rossetti, W. M. "Portraits of Robert Browning. III." *Magazine of Art* (1890): 261–67.

Ryan, Mark B. "The Resurrection of Frederic Myers." *Journal of Transpersonal Psychology* 42, no. 2 (2010): 149–70.

Sharkey, Olive. "Belvedere Restored." *Irish Arts Review* 19, no. 2 (autumn 2002): 128–35.

Sweeney, John L. ed. *The Painter's Eye: Notes and Essays on the Pictorial Arts by Henry James.* London: Rupert Hart-Davis, 1956.

Schultz, Bart. *Henry Sidgwick, Eye of the Universe: An Intellectual Biography.* Cambridge: Cambridge University Press, 2004.

S[idgwick], A[rthur], and E[leanor] M[ary] S[idgwick]. *Henry Sidgwick: A Memoir.* London: Macmillan, 1906.

Slotten, Ross A. *The Heretic in Darwin's Court: The Life of Alfred Russel Wallace.* New York: Columbia University Press, 2004.

Spielmann, M. H. "The Works of Mr. George F. Watts R. A., with a Complete Catalogue of His Pictures." *Pall Mall Gazette*, Extra Number, 22 (1886): 1–32.

———. *Millais and His Works, with Special Reference to the Exhibition at the Royal Academy 1898.* Edinburgh: William Blackwood and Sons, 1898.

Stead, W. T. ed. "The Photographs of the Month." *Review of Reviews* [July? 1890]: 189–92.

———. "Real Ghost Stories." *Review of Reviews*, (December 1891), repr. W. T. Stead, *Real Ghost Stories.* London: Grant Richards, 1892.

Surtees, Virginia. *The Paintings and Drawings of Dante Gabriel Rossetti (1828–1882): A Catalogue Raisonné.* Oxford: Clarendon Press, 1971.

Symonds, John Addington. "Mrs. F. W. H. Myers." *Sun Artists*, no. 7 (April 1891): 51–54.

Taylor, Jenny Bourne, and Sally Shuttleworth, eds. *Embodied Selves: An Anthology of Psychological Texts 1830–1890.* Oxford: Clarendon Press, 1998.

Treuherz, Julian, Elizabeth Prettejohn, and Edwin Becker. *Dante Gabriel Rossetti.* London: Thames and Hudson, 2003. Published in conjunction with an exhibition of the same name at the Walker Art Gallery, Liverpool, October 16, 2003–January 18, 2004, and at the Van Gogh Museum, Amsterdam.

Trodd, Colin, and Stephanie Brown, eds., Representations of *G. F. Watts, Art Making in Victorian Culture*. Aldershot: Ashgate, 2004.

Tromans, Nicholas. *The Art of G. F. Watts*. London: Paul Holberton Publishing, 2017.

Tucker, Keith. *Chronicle of Cadoxton*. Neath: Historical Projects, 1994.

Viscomi, Joseph. "Two Fake Blakes Revisited; One Dew-Smith Revealed." In *Blake in Our Time: Essays in Honour of G. E. Bentley, Jr.*, edited by Karen Mulhallen, 35–78. Toronto: University of Toronto Press, 2010.

Vrettos, Athena. "Displaced Memories in Victorian Fiction and Psychology." *Victorian Studies* 49, no. 2 (winter 2007): 199–207. https://www.jstor.org/stable/4626277

Walkley, Christina. *The Ghost in the Looking Glass: The Victorian Seamstress*. London: Peter Owen, 1981.

Waller, David. *The Magnificent Mrs. Tennant: The Adventurous Life of Gertrude Tennant, Victorian Grande Dame*. New Haven: Yale University Press, 2009.

Walker, Pierre A., and Greg W. Zacharias. *The Complete Letters of Henry James, 1876–1878*. 2 vols. Lincoln: University of Nebraska Press, 2012.

———. *The Complete Letters of Henry James, 1878–1880*. 2 vols. Lincoln: University of Nebraska Press, 2014.

Ward, Chloe. "England's Michelangelo in the Metropolitan Museum of Art: The G. F. Watts Exhibition, 1884–85." *Comparative American Studies* 14, no. 1 (2016): 62–75. https://doi.org/10.1080/14775700.2016.1213019.

Watson, Margaretta Frederick, ed. *Collecting the Pre-Raphaelites: the Anglo-American enchantment*. Aldershot: Ashgate, 1997.

Watts Gallery, Compton. *A Catalogue of the Pictures by G. F. Watts R. A. at the Picture Gallery Compton*. The Picture Gallery Compton Lane Near Guildford, 1904.

Watts, G. F. "The Present Conditions of Art." *Nineteenth Century* (1880), repr. M. S. Watts, Watts Annals 3: 148–90.

———. "On Taste in Dress." *Nineteenth Century* (January 1883): 45–57.

Watts, M. S. *George Frederic Watts: The Annals of An Artist's Life*. 3 vols. London: Macmillan and Co., 1912.

Whittington-Egan, Molly. *Frank Miles and Oscar Wilde: "Such White Lilies."* High Wycombe: Rivendale Press, 2008.

Wilde, Oscar. "The Canterville Ghost." In *The Canterville Ghost, The Happy Prince, and Other Stories*. London: Penguin Books, 2010.

Wildman, Stephen, et al. *Waking Dreams: The Art of the Pre-Raphaelites from the Delaware Art Museum*. Alexandria, VA: Art Services International, 2004. Published in conjunction with an exhibition of the same name organized by Art Services International, Alexandria, VA.

Wilton, Andrew, and Robert Upstone, eds. *The Age of Rossetti, Burne-Jones & Watts. Symbolism in Britain 1860–1910*. London: Tate Gallery Publishing, 1997. Published in conjunction with an exhibition of the same name organized at the Tate Gallery, October 16, 1997–January 4, 1998.

Wolf, Sylvia. *Julia Margaret Cameron's Women*. New Haven: Yale University Press, 1998.

Wolstenholme, Susan. "Possession and Personality: Spiritualism in *The Bostonians*." *American Literature* 49, no. 4 (January 1978): 580–91. https://doi.org/10.2307/2924775.

Yeates, Amelia. "'A Slave Kept in Leyland's Back Parlour': The Male Artist in the Victorian Marketplace." *Visual Culture in Britain* 16 (2): 171–85. https://doi.org/10.1080/14714787.2015.1041814.

Zegher, Catherine de, and Johan De Smet, eds. *Julia Margaret Cameron*. Ghent: Snoeck, 2015. Published in conjunction with the exhibition *Julia Margaret Cameron (1815–1879), Pioneer of Photography* at the Museum voor Schone Kunsten, Ghent, organized by the Victoria and Albert Museum, London, in cooperation with the Museum voor Schone Kunsten, Ghent, March 14–June 14, 2015.

EVY
GEORGE FREDERIC WATTS'S PORTRAIT OF EVELEEN TENNANT

KEDRUN LAURIE | OCCASIONAL PAPER 5

In the 1870s the young Eveleen Tennant was much admired for her beauty and through her mother's London salon frequented some of the best-known artists and writers of the day. The ambitious Mrs Tennant, determined to secure her the best possible match, had her lovely daughter's portrait taken many times over, most notably by J. E. Millais and G. F. Watts.

The painting of her by Watts at the Delaware Art Museum was a favourite of the artist. He was equally fond of and protective towards its sitter. But the picture's girlish simplicity, like that of Eveleen herself, is deceptive.

Presenting much new research and drawing particularly on the uninhibited manuscript journals of Eveleen's sister Dorothy, Kedrun Laurie tells the history of the picture and that of the much-pursued Eveleen, who ended by eluding reductive definitions of her to become an independent photographer, a splendid portraitist in her own right.

KEDRUN LAURIE studied French and English Literature at Girton College, Cambridge and went on to become Assistant Curator of the Geffrye Museum in London. She subsequently worked for some years as a consultant on the restoration of historic parks and gardens. After moving to Belgium in 1989 she received her doctorate from King's College London with a thesis examining how the humanitarian concerns of the Victorian era changed the way in which we write about nature. She now works as an independent scholar in France and publishes on the art and literature of the late nineteenth century.

www.ingramcontent.com/pod-product-compliance
Lightning Source LLC
Chambersburg PA
CBHW040543220526
45473CB00016B/3011